Learning to Love

Learning to Love

Martin Israel
with Neil Broadbent

MOWBRAY
London and New York

Mowbray
A Continuum imprint
The Tower Building, 11 York Road, London, SE1 7NX
370 Lexington Avenue, New York NY 10017-6503

First published 2001

British Library Cataloguing-in-Publication Data
A catalogue record for this book is available from the British Library.

ISBN 0-264-67529-0

Designed and typeset by BookEns Ltd, Royston, Herts
Printed and bound in Great Britain by
TJ International, Padstow, Cornwall

Contents

Foreword

This book aims at introducing the principles of the Christian faith to an intelligent but uncommitted enquirer. Such a person may not have been educated in any religious faith, or alternatively, may have moved from agnosticism to tentative belief in a Higher Power beyond the limits of human reason, through having been deeply affected by some personal experience.

Whether a chapter focuses on a basic tenet of the faith or on our daily response to it, all chapters conclude with a section for further reflection on the topic. Passages are taken from writers old and new. The book ends with a look at additional resources.

The writer's approach is moderately liberal, but friendly to both the evangelical and catholic wings of the Christian church. It acknowledges the importance of dogma, the system of teaching laid down by the church, but avoids any tendency to dogmatism, an arrogant assertion of personal opinion, in the above context a rigid, unyielding theological point of view. Scientific knowledge, though marvellous and never ceasing in new discoveries, simply brings us ever closer to the brink of a 'black hole' of ignorance.

Our life on earth is a mystery, a brief time span during which we may discover that our greatest calling is one of learning to love.

Acknowledgements

The writers are indebted to F. L. Cross and E. A. Livingstone for their great work, *The Oxford Dictionary of the Christian Church*. This is a superb source of information about all details of Christianity, theological terms and Christian writers as well as an enthralling history of the faith.

The biblical quotations are all taken from the Revised English Bible unless other sources are mentioned.

The extract from 'Lord God, Your Love has called us here' (p. 51) is reproduced by kind permission of Stainer & Bell Ltd, and Hope Publishing Company.

1

The foundation of existence: God and creation

God is Love. Whoever sought to define him would be like a blind person trying to count the grains of sand on the sea shore. (John Climacus, *The Ladder of Divine Ascent*)

How do things come to be? What made the hard rock and the fertile soil? The beautiful flower and the fertile crops that sustain animal life? The vast array of animals in the world ruled by the human mind? What fashions this arrogant mind, and guides it by a quiet, informed way? And this is merely one consideration of creation, appertaining to one fairly small planet in an equally small solar system, one of an enormous number of others of its kind.

Here is creation – that has had its beginning beyond our span of knowledge. Cosmologists give the age of our universe as fifteen billion years, and 4500 million years as the time when our particular solar system was fashioned within it. It is very easy to lose our bearings in the vastness of the cosmic scheme, and let it take control of our lives; in fact, unless we brace ourselves for the responsibilities peculiar to human destiny, the forces around us become destructive and work towards our own ruin. The forces of nature are fierce and unremitting even at their calmest. Our survival depends on the generous way in which we work with these powers as well as the self-control we exert in rising above the selfish temptation of harnessing to our own needs the creatures around us, regardless of their own welfare and their special place in the scheme of life.

Is there a personal power intimately concerned in the work of creation, one that faithfully sustains the populous earth with its ebullient life and faithfully enduring framework of air and water, rock and soil? This inanimate planet provides a home for all life; it undergoes a change of attrition over countless centuries, while the life it supports dies continually, and is continually replaced by the reproduction of similar forms. These living organisms multiply, and their progeny may demonstrate various changes in structure, which are inherited, as were the previous forms of life, from the basic pattern of the living creature. This is the process of evolution which is accepted by nearly all scientists, though the mechanism involved may on occasion be hotly disputed.

Who organizes the living activity of the universe? Until about 300 years ago the existence of an all-powerful, beneficent creator was accepted by nearly all educated people, who also attributed the manifest order of creation to this source. But the development of different forms of a single animal or plant in a restricted, enclosed environment was an important indication to many scientists that the process of evolution was germane to life itself, being a simple property of the animal or plant and not requiring any outside agent to promote it. Thus the idea that there can be a rational proof of divine activity has been undermined as people have got wiser about the mechanism of reproduction and the associated workings of nature in the world.

The fact is that any intelligent creative force in the universe will show itself in all natural phenomena, the destructive no less than the beneficial. In other words, death is as much a part of life as is growth and maturation. Death is essential for life because a long-surviving population would prevent the establishment of anything new in the universe. William Blake put it thus:

> Man was made for Joy and Woe;
> And when this we rightly know,
> Thro' the World we safely go,
> Joy and woe are woven fine,
> A clothing for the soul divine.[1]

When anything good or bad befalls us personally, we tend to attribute a personality to the cosmic principle; but when it affects large populations it seems to transcend personality as we know it and assume truly cosmic, or universal, proportions.

A great truth about God is contained in the medieval mystical treatise *The Cloud of Unknowing*: 'He can be taken and held by love but not by thought.'[2] When we are open in love, to even one person, God enters our consciousness also. When we strain after God with our mind only, the door slams shut in our face. When we are open to life and enjoying each moment of it in guileless happiness, God is close to us in the company of those we meet in the present. If our mind is clouded with ulterior desires, these have no difficulty in occluding the divine vision from our gaze.

Is the God of happiness and contentment I have delineated a real being or merely an emotional release? Inasmuch as we feel rested in his company it seems to show that the divine image revealed in this way is close to the root of our personality. The revelation comes to those who are ready to receive it, who do not have a selfish desire to be in charge of circumstances.

To the person of spiritual depth, whom we call a mystic, God is closer to their inner being (or soul) than their personality (their distinctive character). A human personal contact is usually sudden and fleeting, but a divine encounter persists, and acts as a source of illumination that blazes a trail of renewed living and blessing to those in its range. Those who have been thus infused hail the holiness of the encounter. Usually the bare experience is anonymous, but if the person experiencing it is deeply religious, they may identify it with the founder or a mighty exemplar of their faith.

Proof of the existence of a divine principle which is called God is essentially private and personal. One has felt one's inner being lifted up in unexplained exultation which extends to the limits of the universe, and is in unity with that universe. In this state of being one is joyful, 'for while having nothing, we possess all things'.[3] It is in fact impossible to define God, because whatever we say is inadequate. The divine principle is far beyond finite human understanding. Thus we are forbidden to depict God in any physical form and worship it.[4] Yet the next of the Ten Commandments forbids us to misuse the name of God.[5]

This name is written in Hebrew characters as YHWH in the Old Testament, and was probably pronounced 'Yahweh', but the name was regarded as too sacred to be uttered, and was replaced by alternative words, *adonai* ('Lord') or *elohim* ('God'), to warn readers to use one of these in its place. Religion that accepts a supernaturally revealed God who sustains a personal relation with his creatures is described as *theistic*, and *theism* is a belief in such a God. By contrast, *deism* is belief in the existence of a supreme being arising from reason rather than revelation. In other words, deism stems from the human mind in an attempt to explain the enigma of creation. As more and more of the enigma is elucidated by that mind through scientific research, so the supreme being recedes in prominence and deism is edged out into atheism.

The principal monotheistic faiths spring from a Semitic root: Judaism, which is the basis of both Christianity and Islam. The strength of theism is the personal contact which the rational creature enjoys with the creator; but its weakness is the temptation to reduce that creator to human stature, to a person who has special favourites, like the children of Israel in Old Testament times. When misfortune strikes a group, they may yield to the expedient of blaming a suspect denomination for offending God, and vicious persecution may follow. The history of the three monotheistic religions is full of terrible examples of this. It follows that religion should be practised by emotionally balanced, educated people who realize that the enigmas of life may be borne with faith but are transcended only by knowledge.

Upon Reflection

God, as considered in himself, in his holy being, before anything is brought forth by him or out of him, is only an eternal will to all goodness. This is the one eternal, immutable God, that from eternity to eternity changes not, that can be neither more nor less nor anything else but an eternal will to all the goodness that is in himself and can come from him. The creation of ever so many worlds or systems of creatures adds nothing to, nor takes anything from, this immutable God. He always was and always will be the same immutable will to all goodness. So that as certainly as he is the creator, so certainly he is the blesser of every created thing, and can give nothing but blessing, goodness, and happiness from himself, because he has in himself nothing else to give. It is much more possible for the sun to give forth darkness than for God to do or be, or give forth anything but blessing and goodness.

William Law (1686–1761), *The Spirit of Love* [6]

To find or know God in reality, by any outward proofs, or by anything but by God himself made manifest and self-evident in you, will never be your case either here or hereafter. For neither God, nor heaven, nor hell, nor the devil, nor the world and the flesh, can be any otherwise knowable in you, or by you, but by their own existence and manifestation in you. And all pretended knowledge of any of these things, beyond or without this self-evident sensibility of their birth within you, is only such knowledge of them as the blind man has of that light that never entered into him.

William Law, *The Way to Divine Knowledge* [7]

2

Jesus: servant and Christ

The Son of God was made man so that man might become son of God.
(Irenaeus of Lyons, *Against Heresies*)

The life and ministry of Jesus is described in the four Gospels. The first three, those of St Matthew, St Mark and St Luke, are so alike that they can, in many passages, be placed side by side and viewed as it were at a glance. Hence they are called *synoptic*, which means 'at one glance'. The fourth Gospel, that of St John, gives a different account of Jesus' ministry. The eyewitness, 'the disciple whom Jesus loved, is unnamed. Despite the attribution to St John there are good reasons for doubting whether he was the same person as the apostle mentioned in Mark 3.17, Matthew 4.21 and Luke 5.10.

The life of Jesus is a compound of spiritual strength, charismatic (or psychic) power and miracle. How this is interpreted depends on the theological stance of the individual. The orthodox believer will accept the biblical account in faith whether in obedience to Catholic doctrine or Evangelical adherence to scriptural teaching. The liberal believer gives a loyal place to reason (or common sense), explaining the miraculous element of the Bible as legend, misunderstood natural phenomena or the superstitious misinterpretation of unusual events in the life of the person, whether the heroes of the Old Testament or Jesus and those who followed him.

The Life of Jesus

Jesus was born about 5 or 4 BC, of the Virgin Mary. She was betrothed to Joseph, but Jesus was conceived before they came to live together. The birth narratives are found in Matthew's and Luke's Gospels only, and the circumstances attending Jesus' birth are quite distinct in each account. Except for Luke's picturesque account of the 12-year-old Jesus remaining in the Temple after his parents and their party had left for home after the feast of the Passover, we do not meet Jesus until the time of his baptism by John the Baptist, who appears in all four Gospels. After that, his ministry began and his activity knew no cessation until his crucifixion some three years later.

The Work of Jesus

HEALING. This was probably Jesus' principal work. The Holy Spirit emanated from him like water flowing from a fountain. Jesus could make instantaneous communication with those who were in need. Both his innate love and his psychic sensitivity made his capacity to relate to people of both sexes and many different religious and racial groups a miraculous aspect of his personality. True healing is always divine, for it is God alone, by the Holy Spirit, who effects healing, whether of the body or the mind. Jesus, in uniting the Father and the Holy Spirit, was the perfect agent in a healing ministry.

TEACHING. The word of life proceeded from Jesus' lips. The most comprehensive collection of his teaching is contained in the Sermon on the Mount.[1] It commences with nine beatitudes and continues with instruction about living in the spirit of God's kingdom, the proper practice of the laws of the Old Testament, detachment from wealth, love of one's neighbour, and a will set to fulfil entry to God's kingdom. The depth of compassion and the understanding of human weakness in this teaching is like a fresh breeze blowing on the harsh judgementalism of much of the morality of the Old Testament, yet there is no trace of permissiveness. Jesus had too great a respect for humans, despite their frequent ignorance of what they were doing, to lapse into sentimental forgiveness without the strongest warning not to persist in destructive, self-centred ways of living. The wage of sin is death in the words of St Paul,[2] but cold, obsessive, unforgiving attitudes may be closer to death than warmer ones that can relax and accommodate the sinner in their love. Jesus' teaching flowed from a fine mind, but it was fed by a heart that vibrated in sympathy with every human mood and suffered in solidarity with every human weakness. His frequent encounters with the dregs of humanity, and the glorious hope his forgiveness bestowed on them, contrasted tellingly with the unqualified condemnation he visited on those who wallowed in religious devotion but whose private lives belied their beliefs. The twenty-third chapter of Matthew's Gospel is a massive tirade against the contemporary scribes and Pharisees. Their hypocrisy was of monumental proportions and they were concerned principally about their own welfare. There were, of course, exceptions like Gamaliel, a Pharisee who counselled a liberal policy towards the earliest Christian community.[3]

EXORCISM. The casting out of evil spirits was an important part of Jesus' ministry. These spirits may have been fallen angels or the souls of evil, unrepentant humans who were no longer alive in the flesh. The most spectacular account of Jesus' power as an exorcist was seen when he relieved two men in the country of the Gadarenes who were possessed by demons. He drove the demons out into a herd of pigs, who rushed over the edge into a lake and perished in the water.[4] One cannot avoid sparing a little sympathy for the pigs, who appeared not to deserve this fate.

THE DEATH OF JESUS. A charismatic figure of the stature of Jesus was bound to inflame envy among professional religionists like many of the scribes and Pharisees. Their disapproval of his willingness to perform healing acts on the Sabbath is typical, as is their objection to his indifference to the dietary laws.[5] The Pharisees soon began to plot against Jesus, discussing how to destroy him.[6] An additional factor in their hostility may have been the popularity evoked by Jesus amongst the common people, who might make him a focus of insurrection against Caesar.[7]

The people themselves hung on his words and rejoiced over his deeds, but he deliberately refused to lead an insurrection against the Romans, thus dashing the hopes of the very people who revered him most. His triumphal entry into Jerusalem, riding on a donkey, with the crowd shouting: 'Hosanna to the Son of David! Blessed is he who comes in the name of the Lord! Hosanna in the heavens!'[8] ended with their shouts of 'Crucify him!'[9] soon after.

A characteristic form of Jesus' teaching was the parable, a narrative of imagined events used to illustrate a moral or spiritual lesson. Matthew 13 is devoted almost entirely to a parabolic account of the literally indescribable kingdom of Heaven. A further account is contained in Matthew 25, spoken at the very end of Jesus' life, in which he laid down some of the requirements before we can enter that kingdom: alertness, enterprise and concern for other people as well as oneself.

A pivotal event in Jesus' life was the Passover meal in the year AD 30. He ate it with the twelve apostles whom he had chosen at the beginning of his ministry,[10] and in the course of the meal, in the accounts of the three synoptic Gospels, he instituted the Eucharist. In John's account there is no Eucharist, but instead Jesus washes the feet of the disciples and then, foretelling Judas Iscariot's treachery, proceeds with the glorious 'farewell discourses' and ends with his magnificent priestly prayer.[11] (There is in fact more than a little allusion to the Eucharist in John 6.)

After supper Jesus and the apostles left for the Mount of Olives where Jesus foretold Peter's imminent disowning of him, and then they came to Gethsemane, a small olive garden, where he went to pray. His anguish was severe, for he knew by this time what fate confronted him. Meanwhile the disciples slept soundly. He bade them wake up as Judas arrived with a large company of men to arrest him. He submitted calmly and was taken to the high priest Caiaphas' house where he was interrogated by the Sanhedrin, the highest court of justice and the supreme council in ancient Jerusalem. In the course of this questioning he claimed to be the Son of Man seated at the right hand of the Almighty, who would come with the clouds of heaven. This was tantamount to claiming that he was the Messiah (or Christ) and divine, and it caused a commotion. The high priest judged that this was blasphemy and that Jesus should be put to death,[12] but only the Roman governor Pontius Pilate could authorize this. When Pilate questioned Jesus he got no reply whatsoever. He would have preferred to release Jesus, for he knew that it was out of malice that Jesus had been handed over to him. But the crowd were insistent that Jesus be crucified, choosing the release of the criminal Barabbas instead of him. And so Jesus was led out to be crucified, at nine in the morning. Two robbers were crucified with him.

At midday a darkness fell over the whole land, which lasted until three in the afternoon, at which time Jesus died. Pilate gave permission to a sympathetic follower, Joseph of Arimathaea, to take the body away. Joseph took the body from the cross, wrapped him in a sheet, laid him in a tomb cut out of the rock, and rolled a stone across the entrance.[13] Mark's account probably ends at 16.8 when

Mary of Magdala, Mary the mother of James, and Salome brought spices, intending to anoint him, and were dumbfounded to find the stone already rolled back and a young man sitting on the right-hand side, wearing a white robe. The women were told that Jesus was not there, because he had been raised, and that they should tell his disciples and Peter that he was going ahead of them into Galilee. The remainder of the chapter, which is little more than a summary of the appearances of the risen Christ, is not present in some of the most ancient copies of the book.

The other three Gospels give vivid accounts of the risen Christ. The main appearance recorded by Luke is especially memorable. Two people walking to a village called Emmaus encountered a stranger on the way as they continued their melancholy debate about Jesus' tragic end, and how some women had failed to find the body in the tomb but had seen a vision of angels that affirmed that he was alive. Then the stranger broke in and explained all the Old Testament references to the Messiah. When they reached the village the stranger made as if to continue his journey, but his companions pressed him to stay. He obliged them, and when seated at table with them he took the bread and pronounced the blessing. He offered it to them, and their eyes were opened so that they recognized him, but he vanished from their sight. They said 'Were not our hearts on fire as he talked with us on the road and explained the scriptures to us?'[14]

The Nature of Jesus

The doctrine of the Trinity is the central dogma of Christian theology. It states that the one God exists in three Persons and one substance: Father, Son and Holy Spirit. God is one, yet self-differentiated. The God who reveals himself to humanity is one God equally in three distinct modes of existence, but remains one through all eternity. In this scheme Jesus Christ is Son of God. This type of language is obviously metaphorical, for God has no private family. Rather, all creatures are part of a universal holy family.

How much is it necessary to believe every detail of the miraculous element underpinning the life of Jesus, especially the virgin birth, the bodily resurrection, and the more extravagant episodes like the calming of the storm,[15] the multiplication of the loaves,[16] and Jesus and Peter walking on the water?[17] Orthodox believers will accept all this in loyal faith, but liberals will be dissatisfied. Only direct proof will convince them, and this is not possible in investigating events that occurred two millennia ago. It is a principle of science that repeatability is a prerequisite in proving the truth of an alleged phenomenon. The scientific approach therefore is inappropriate in this case.

Jesus was certainly so exceptional a man, with so many spiritual gifts, that it is no wonder that deity was attributed to him. The orthodox homage is well justified. But he was also very human, with emotional reactions common to other people. He was angry when the Temple was used for commercial purposes that exceeded the bounds needed for pilgrims to purchase sacrificial victims necessary for oblations.[18] He was in agony when he was crucified and cried out, 'My God, my God, why have you forsaken me?'[19]

It is evident that such an outstanding person as Jesus may elicit such conflicting reactions as uncritical acceptance and measured respect. What ultimately matters is the change of heart that he called forth in those around him, and in the many millions of people from his time to the present. The essential proof of his resurrection is the resurrection of the shattered disciples from spiritual death to new life as they broadcast the Good News (or gospel) to the world. It is wiser to stress the humanity of Jesus than his deity, for his work will always be with humans. We all have a spark of the divine in us, though sinful attitudes may conceal it until we learn better conduct. Jesus had so close a connection with God that it is not unreasonable to call him God's Son.

Upon Reflection

Ask what God is? His name is Love; he is the good, the perfection, the peace, the joy, the glory, and the blessing of every life. Ask what Christ is? He is the universal remedy of all evil broken forth in nature and creature. He is the destruction of misery, sin, darkness, death and hell. He is the resurrection and life of all fallen nature. He is the unwearied compassion, the long-suffering pity, the never-ceasing mercifulness of God to every want and infirmity of human nature. He is the breathing-forth of the heart, life, and spirit of God, into all the dead race of Adam. He is the seeker, the finder, the restorer of all that was lost and dead to the life of God. He is the Love that from Cain to the end of time prays for all murderers, the Love that willingly suffers and dies among thieves that thieves may have a life with him in paradise; the Love that visits publicans, harlots, and

sinners, and wants and seeks to forgive where most is to be forgiven
. . .

William Law, *The Spirit of Prayer* [20]

The meaning of the Incarnation, therefore, is simply that we do not
have to *attain* union with God. Man does not have to climb to the
infinite and become God, because, out of love, the infinite God
descends to the finite and becomes man. Despite man's refusal of God,
despite his pride, his fear, his helpless and hopeless involvement in the
vicious circle of sin, God's nature remains unalterably love – the *agape*
which consists in giving oneself wholly and without reservation to the
beloved. Therefore the eternal Word, the Logos, becomes flesh,
making our nature his nature; he assumes our limitations, suffers our
pains and dies our death. More than this, he bears the burden of our
sins: that is, he remains in union with us even though we crucify him
and spit on him; he continues to dwell within us and to offer, or
sacrifice, our lives to God even though we commit every imaginable
form of depravity. In short, God has wedded himself to humanity, has
united his divine essence with our inmost being 'for better for worse,
for richer for poorer, in sickness and in health' for all eternity, even
though we elect to be damned.

> *If I ascend up into heaven, thou art there;*
> *If I make my bed in hell, behold, thou are there also.*

All that remains for us to do is to say, 'Yes – Amen' to this tremendous
fact, and this is still within the power of our fallen nature. Our motive
for saying it, however perverted by pride and fear, makes not the least
difference, because the fact is the fact: we have been given union with
God whether we like it or not, want it or not, know it or not. Our flesh
has become his flesh, and we cannot jump out of our own skins. And
once we realize the futility of our pride, that we can neither ascend to
God nor, by reason of pride, prevent his descent to us, the proud core
of egoism is simply dissolved – overwhelmed by God's love. The
function of Christian morality and spirituality is not to earn or deserve
this gift of eternal life, but rather to appreciate and express it. The saint
is holy not to attain union with God, but to give thanks for it.

Alan Watts, *Behold the Spirit* [21]

Christ given for us is Christ given into us.

William Law, *The Spirit of Love* [22]

We can achieve this only through the spirit of prayer: 'Everything calls
for it, everything is to be done in it and governed by it.' Ask not
therefore how shall we enter into this Religion of Love and Salvation?

for it is itself entered into us, it has taken Possession of us from the Beginning. It is *Immanuel* in every human Soul; it lies as a Treasure of Heaven, and Eternity in us; it cannot be divided from us by the Power of Man; we cannot lose it ourselves; it will never leave us nor forsake us.

William Law, *The Spirit of Prayer* [23]

3

The Holy Spirit: the Lord, the Giver of Life

If you live according to the sinful nature, you will die; but if by the Spirit you put to death the misdeeds of the body, you will live. (Romans 8.13)

The Holy Spirit is the fundamental life-giving power in creation. He is distinct from the Father and the Son, but of the same substance and coequal and coeternal with them. He can most easily be regarded as the mode of action of God in the universe.

He plays a role in Scripture as an instrument of divine action, both in nature and in the human heart. Thus in the creation narrative the Spirit hovered over the surface of the water,[1] he inspired the artistic mastery of Bezalel,[2] the military prowess of Joshua,[3] and Samson's legendary strength.[4] The Spirit was bestowed on those whose work was to communicate divine truth, like the prophets,[5] or to exhibit moral excellence.[6] The Spirit was especially to inspire the coming Davidic King,[7] and the servant of the Lord.[8] It was predicted that in the future there would be a great extension of the Spirit's work and power.[9] The Spirit was also the bestower of intellectual ability, filling the devout and conveying wisdom and religious knowledge.[10]

The Holy Spirit played a great part in the baptism of Jesus[11] and was responsible for driving him into the wilderness where he remained for forty days tempted by Satan.[12] Jesus' conception was attributed to the operation of the Holy Spirit.[13] But the Spirit was comparatively unavailable until Jesus' death and resurrection. In the course of the Farewell Discourses of the fourth Gospel, the Spirit was called 'another Comforter', distinct from Jesus, whom he succeeded while doing similar works and fulfilling all that Jesus had said and performed.[14] Indeed, Paul could call the Spirit 'the Spirit of Jesus',[15] almost identical with Jesus.[16] Possessing the Spirit made one active in Christian worship,[17] proclamation and instruction,[18] and in moral discernment.[19] The Spirit was also operative in raising Christian believers after death to the form of spiritual bodies,[20] which were portrayed as living mortal bodies in Romans 8.11. The Holy Spirit was also called the 'Paraclete' or 'Advocate'.

The Manifestation of the Holy Spirit

How does one know whether the Holy Spirit is directly inspiring oneself in everyday life? Of the three members of the Holy Trinity he is certainly the closest to humanity as a whole. It is held that the mode of the Spirit's procession in the Godhead is by way of 'spiration', not 'generation', and that this procession takes place as from a single principle. The word 'spiration' indicates a breathing action, firm and continuous. The Spirit is known by an expansion in a person's consciousness. In this there is a release from fear and hatred and an openness in warmth to those around one, and to all people in general. Negative emotions are occluded if not obliterated, and one is lifted up in joy.

A person who is inspired by the Spirit is also filled with a burning desire to act creatively. This action is not primarily egocentric but tends to be imbued with a more expansive purpose. It is concerned with humanity collectively, though a certain degree of self-esteem may show itself to the aware individual. The creative genius of great composers, artists and writers is induced by the Spirit, as is also brilliant extempore preaching and public speaking. The prerequisite for Spirit-directed activity is a submerging of the personality in devotion to God, in whom all creation is subsumed. The word 'charismatic' is frequently used in connection with a specific type of worship characterized by spontaneity, ecstatic utterance and exuberant claims of divine inspiration. The proof of this exalted claim to be 'filled with the Spirit' lies in the character of the individual and not in their mode of worship; if they feel in any way superior to the common run of humanity they proclaim their own inadequacy. On the other hand, they are fully entitled to their own opinions and ways of worship.

Jesus himself did not exhibit such 'charismatic' phenomena in order to draw attention to himself, but the Holy Spirit could not remain hidden in him, because of his burning participation in the life of the world, especially its suffering. It can be said almost as a rule that exhibitionistic behaviour demeans the work of the Holy Spirit while elevating the self-regard of the individual to grotesque proportions. All truly devout believers repudiate this tendency absolutely, but there are few who have the strength of character to resist the insidious impact of flattery. Jesus condemned those who called him 'Lord, Lord,' without the words touching them. Only those who did the will of his heavenly Father, he said, would enter the kingdom of Heaven. Not even such charismatic gifts as prophecy, exorcism and miracle-working would automatically gain them divine recognition if the disposition of their heart was faulty, i.e. if they did not do the will of the Father.[21]

The Fruits of the Spirit

These are spiritual in nature. Spirituality is the practice of the holiness inherent in life, whereby the dense material structure of the world is transformed into a glowing edifice within which the divine nature manifests itself. This holiness shows itself primarily in life itself, for living forms adapt themselves to their environment and grow in it. They, in turn, influence the environment. It is the privilege of humans to possess moral sensitivity, knowing the difference between right and wrong. By acting accordingly, they effect a cardinal influence.

The fruits, or harvest, of the Holy Spirit are nine in number: love, joy, peace, patience, kindness, goodness, fidelity, gentleness and self-control.[22] These should be the basis of all law from the civic to the international. Non-human forms of life appear to have no intrinsic morality; they can take care of their own at best, but later have little family loyalty. Humans are capable of deep caring, but also, as the twentieth century has revealed in shocking truth, of cruelty unparalleled in sheer vindictiveness. The toll exacted from religious enthusiasm and intolerance has from time immemorial been enormous, so much so that many people are compulsively irreligious. Yet, atheistic systems like communism have not brought any noticeable happiness in their wake. The concept of God, at its very least, serves to raise human consciousness from self-centredness to concern for other people and the greater world.

The Gifts of the Spirit

These are discussed authoritatively in 1 Corinthians 12. They are wise speech, putting the deepest knowledge into words, faith, gifts of healing, miraculous powers, prophecy, the ability to distinguish true spirits from false, the gift of tongues of various kinds, and the ability to interpret them. Like the harvest of the Spirit they come from the same source, and in all of them the same God is active. In each person the Holy Spirit is to be at work for some useful purpose. The gifts of the Spirit are more immediately manifest to the world at large, whereas the fruits of the Spirit are intimate expansions of awareness that lead to progressive spiritual growth of the person. This indeed ought to be the way of personal actualization: inner spiritual illumination followed by the emergence of spiritual gifts in the world.

Whereas the harvest of the Spirit is entirely life-giving and beneficial, some of the gifts, especially those last on the list above, are ambivalent. They may inflate the self-esteem if this has not previously been purified by the fruits of the Spirit. Spiritual gifts can promote spectacular psychical phenomena, the value of which depends on the discernment of the individual. Pentecostalism is the Christian denomination in which the gifts of the Spirit are most enthusiastically cultivated and their effects used. A limitation of this type of approach is its non-rational attitude to the deeper problems of humanity and its stress on the power of evil spirits. If the rationalist tends to reduce human evil to genetic and environmental factors, the charismatic believer may be largely fixated on the independent power of evil transmitted by false spirits. Admittedly evil cosmic powers are depicted graphically in such Bible passages as Ephesians 6.10–18 and 1 Peter 5.8–11, but such an approach can lead to a damaging superstitious fear and also to hostility towards anyone who appears to be unusual. Various unpopular groups have been victimized on this pretext, and many people have been killed as a result of fear activating an underlying religious or racial prejudice. No one should enter the field of exorcism (deliverance) until they are mature in their attitude to themselves and to the world. Extreme views are dangerous.

St Paul's placing of spiritual gifts is instructive. First come apostles, then prophets, then teachers, miracle-workers, those with healing gifts, those who are able to help or guide others, and finally the gift of tongues.[23] This last, also called *glossolalia*, is the power of praying, especially praising God, under the action of the Spirit and under the pressure of ecstasy. It leads to the making of sounds which, though continuous and syllabled, are not intelligible as language. It plays an important part in charismatic worship, but in fact it is of limited value unless there is someone present who can interpret it to the congregation. The gift of tongues is most valuable in private worship when it is often a means of opening the person to the presence of God and so deepening their prayer. In public worship, St Paul commends speaking five intelligible words, for the benefit of others as well as oneself, rather than thousands of words in the language of ecstasy.[24]

The Spirit of Service

The essence of Christian service is the art of the three-way conversation. Skill in service, like any other skill, grows with practice. Being a group activity in which the participants are God, oneself and any others, there are always present both the openly acknowledged agenda and also a hidden set of intentions and wishes. 'For my thoughts are not your thoughts, nor are your ways my ways', as the prophet Isaiah declared long ago.[25]

Since the purpose of this life is that we may grow in love and usefulness to our neighbour, a prerequisite is inner knowledge of our own strengths and weaknesses. Since we are to incarnate divine love and compassion in our souls and bodies, we need a continuing overshadowing by the Holy Spirit, so that we may think only those thoughts that the Lord would have us think, speak only those words that God would have us express, and do only those deeds that conform with his desire for our wholeness and holiness.

The Easter people are those who know the power of Christ and his resurrection because they have gone through their own Gethsemane, crucifixion and harrowing of their own inner hell, and have been raised up by God to a new life based much less on conforming to the powers of this world. Social custom and expectations, unspoken group fears and resentments and other silent difficulties recede, with much more emphasis on the Truth that sets us free.

'Every member service' is right; it always has been, and is a necessary antidote to past overdoses of clerical authority. But it is Christian service only to the extent that every participant in the 'group expression' has set aside self-concern, self-protection, self-aggrandizement and all fears of self (because sin is self-will), and has the purity of heart to will only that which God desires.

This may seem a theory, a theology, too far beyond people like us, but in practice this is not so. The more inner freedom we have to pay attention to what is actually happening in us, around us, and in our community and other groupings, the more clearly we can see not only how we are functioning but also how God is at work in us. And 'absolutely unmixed attention is prayer'.[26] To love God more dearly, see him more clearly, and follow him more nearly, we need, like pygmies, to stand on the shoulders of giants who have gone before us: the great men and women of prayer who have glorified the church's past.

Sharing in the communion of such saints we are strengthened inwardly in the struggle to reduce the power of the seven deadly sins in us. As we 'hear all, see all and say next to nowt', we are empowered, not with potentially self-inflating charismata but with the fruits of the Holy Spirit: love, joy, peace, and the other six enumerated earlier on in the chapter.

Our service improves as, along with John the Baptist, Mary, Jesus and St Paul, we continue to pray, 'Your will be done, O Lord, not mine, on earth as it is in heaven.'

Upon Reflection

The Spirit thus anoints all who seek consciously to live in Christ and thereby become other 'Christs', at once saved and saviours, to be set apart to work for the salvation of the world.

Olivier Clément, *The Roots of Christian Mysticism* [27]

Ask nothing of God, then, but this gift of divine Love, that is, the Holy Spirit. For among all the gifts of God there is none so good and valuable, so noble or so excellent as this. For in no other gift of God save this gift of Love is the Giver Himself the Gift, so that it is the noblest and best of all.

Walter Hilton (fourteenth century), *The Ladder of Perfection* [28]

If I can forget even for a moment all the injuries that have been done to me, and all the unpleasant things people have said about me, and all my fears and worries about the future, if I can start to forgive all those in my life who have betrayed and injured me − always bearing in mind the injury I have done to others − I repeat, if all this incubus of resentment, fear, and hatred which is part of the human condition and is what we call the hell in our existence, can be relieved and cleansed through the power of love, I can suddenly begin to live properly and realize that I am not really alone at all. I will see that both my misery and my hope are part of the universal scheme of becoming, and that I can only begin to be a proper person when I am no longer enclosed in myself. Then I will know that I am part of a greater whole which is the psychic component of all created things. At that point a new awareness comes into me and I begin to understand the meaning of forgiveness. When I am unforgiven– and this was the state of man before the Resurrection – I am enclosed and alone, full of fear, self-justification, and many other fruitless, destructive emotional attitudes. But once this enclosedness is penetrated through love that comes to me, not because I deserve it, but because I am a creature of God, an opening occurs in my defences so that this love can enter me and healing can come to me. This is precisely how people are made whole in Christ. I repeat, once this protective separateness in me is rent asunder by love and I am no longer frightened and resentful, the power of God can come to me and I can begin to realize the Christ within me.

Martin Israel, *Christ, Son of God* [29]

4

The religious quest: the search for truth

In reality holiness consists in one thing alone, namely, fidelity to God's plan. (Jean-Pierre de Caussade)

Pilate asked, 'What is truth?'[1] This rhetorical question came at the end of his interrogation of Jesus. Jesus had replied to a charge brought against him by his fellow Jews. They claimed he was a dangerous criminal who deserved to be put to death, but that they were not allowed to execute anyone themselves.[2] Jesus remained silent before Pilate, but eventually stated that his kingdom did not belong to this world. If it did, he said, his followers would be fighting to save him from the clutches of his own people. In fact, his task was to bear witness to the truth. He was born for this purpose; for this he came into the world, and all who were not deaf listened to his voice.[3] The philosopher Francis Bacon famously wrote, 'What is truth? said jesting Pilate, and would not stay for an answer.'[4]

The religious quest is the supreme search for truth and is unlikely ever to come to an end. This quest investigates the vitally important areas of human living. A life that does not grapple with these matters is destined to boring futility even if it is encompassed with wealth, power and social distinction. Why are we here? What happens to us when we die? Can we in truth know the intentions of a possible Creator God? Worldly success is of transient duration, since we are all served by only a weak body. Indeed, why is this body so easily hurt in the general run of everyday life? Surely the Creator could have fashioned a more endurable human frame, one that was relatively insensitive to pain and capable of much more effort and service.

Religious assurance has been drastically swept out of the limelight by an attitude of doubt and agnosticism, fostered on the one hand by the tumultuous expansion of scientific knowledge and on the other by the tendency to arrogant exclusiveness that characterizes much orthodox religion. While the positive role the church has played over the centuries in promoting education among the general public is laudable, there has also been a considerable tendency to suppress scientific investigation by dogmatic groups who use religion to enforce their own authority to the extent of silencing all other insights into truth. The ambivalent attitude of some types of religious orthodoxy to the theory of evolution is a case in point. While scientific research strongly favours the evolution of earlier forms of a species to the current more complex representative, the view that the various living organisms originate from direct acts of divine creation, as in the biblical account,[5] a view called *creationism*, is canvassed by the religious fundamentalist.

At the end of the twentieth century we can survey how scientific research has split open vast areas of ignorance and darkness. It has placed in human hands the ambivalent power of controlling the world so that it could be transformed into either a veritable garden of Eden [6] or, much more likely, a vale of terrible desolation.[7] The basis of this fearful foreboding is the history of the human race; dark and so often viciously destructive of its earlier spiritual heritage.

To put this foreboding in an adequate perspective, it is useful to return to a fundamental teaching of traditional Christianity, that we are reconciled with God through Jesus' sacrificial death on the cross. This fundamental doctrine of the Christian faith is called the *Atonement*, as in at-one-ment. It is based on God's absolute righteousness, to which nothing impure or sinful can approach. Atonement was represented in the Old Testament in an act of God himself. This might be by the appointment of the sacrificial system through which uncleanness, both ritual and moral, may be purged by the shedding of blood,[8] by a new divine gift to replace the old covenant with a new one,[9] or by the action of a divinely sent 'Servant of the Lord'.[10]

As recorded in the New Testament, Jesus, like John the Baptist, began his ministry with a summons to universal repentance for sin,[11] sin being self-will. He proclaimed the uselessness of blood-sacrifice as a substitute for repentance,[12] yet he spoke of giving his life as a ransom for many.[13] When he instituted the Eucharist he declared the shedding of his blood to constitute 'the new covenant'[14] and to be 'for the forgiveness of sins'.[15] He also applied to himself the words of Isaiah 53 relating to the Suffering Servant.[16] In the fourth Gospel Jesus is represented as 'the Lamb of God who takes away the sin of the world',[17] and his death is shown in terms of sacrifice by being placed side by side with the sacrifice of the paschal lamb at the Passover.[18] Hence his death was already proclaimed to be 'for our sins',[19] and his work expounded on the basis of Isaiah 53.[20]

The early Christians followed St Paul's elaboration of the doctrine. Jesus' death and resurrection were the means by which we are redeemed from the effects of the Law and its transgression (which is sin), from God's condemnation and from death. By baptism the believer mystically shares Christ's death and his victory over it (the resurrection), and acquires, by God's grace (free gift), a new status of sonship, or justification. Peace was made between God and humans 'through the shedding of his blood upon the cross'.[21] Hence, the death of Jesus was an expiation,[22] the means by which at-one-ment is made. The believer is also said to be 'set free by Christ's precious blood'.[23]

The church Fathers took up and followed the doctrine of the New Testament. Origen believed that Jesus' death was a 'ransom' paid to Satan, who had acquired rights over the human as a consequence of the Fall, but was deceived into believing he could hold the sinless Christ. One important view, of St Athanasius, is that God the Son, by taking our nature upon him, has effected a change in human nature as such. This is typified in such a saying as St Athanasius', 'He became human that we might be made divine.'[24] The general patristic teaching is that Christ is our representative, not our substitute; and his resurrection extends to the whole of humanity and beyond.

In the eleventh and twelfth centuries St Anselm shifted the emphasis: the concept of ransom gave way to the idea of 'satisfaction'. No finite being, human or angel, can offer such satisfaction. It was necessary that an infinite being, in other words God himself, should take the place of the human and, by his death, make complete satisfaction to divine justice. Hence the death of Jesus was not a ransom paid to the devil but a debt paid to the Father. Peter Abelard, on the other hand, sought the explanation in terms of 'love'. Christ's atoning death was effective primarily as the final proof of a love for the human which evokes a response of love in the sinner.

The Reformers of the sixteenth century, particularly Martin
Luther and John Calvin, taught that Jesus, in bearing by voluntary
'substitution' the punishment due to the human, was reckoned by
God a sinner in their place. In reaction against the exaggerations of
this 'penal theory' there arose the doctrine which denied the objective
efficacy of the cross and looked upon the death of Jesus as primarily an
example to his followers. And so the debate continues, for the subject
is beyond mere human thinking.

Theological dogma often tells us more about the character of
individuals who wield considerable (though inevitably limited)
power than about eternal truth. The limitation placed on the power
of individual opinion is based on the transience of human life. But
one thing is certain: even the prophets of Old Testament times
insisted that without repentance the offering of sacrifice for sins was
futile.[25] Grace is of divine origin, but though a free gift it is never
cheap. It is fulfilled by the hard work of the recipient. As the
medieval mystic Meister Eckhart put it: 'God can no more do
without us than we can do without him.' It is indeed 'a terrifying
thing to fall into the hands of the living God'.[26] This warning is
especially true of the person who has 'trampled underfoot the Son of
God' and 'insulted God's gracious Spirit', but it has to be taken in due
earnestness by the individual who has been granted an intimation of
the life ahead of them. It is bound to be a life of service, quite possibly
tinctured by a degree of suffering.

It is by following in the way of the great spiritual geniuses of
humanity that we leave the dirt track of squalid lust and enter the
broad highway that leads in the direction of God. This journey,
which is the spiritual quest, is inevitably silent and individual. As
Jesus taught in the Sermon on the Mount, 'You cannot serve God
and Money.'[27] In this respect money stands for the things of this
world. This does not mean isolating oneself from the concerns of the
world, which is potentially as selfish as craving for them, but being
able to detach oneself from a desire to possess them apart from the
bare necessities of civilized life in company with other people. There
is indeed a place for the hermit, one who lives alone in solitude, but
this is an unusual type and not to be regarded as necessarily more
spiritual than those who live in community. The same judgement
applies to these as compared with those who have family
commitments. The test is always the same: are we doing our work
satisfactorily? Those who live in community have an opportunity to

serve people on a wider, yet deeper level than those who are committed to their family. The rationale for committing oneself to a religious community life is service to the world in prayer, which may be widened by teaching, nursing or some other form of activity in the locality. The way of the hermit is one of constant prayer, which may be expanded to the spiritual direction of people on their way to a knowledge of God.

The way to this knowledge is by the intricacies of the Atonement. As we have already seen, we are reconciled with God by the way of Jesus' sacrificial death on the cross. It is dependent on God's grace and the active will, or hard work, of the recipient. As our will is activated, so we see truth on a deeper level than the purely mundane.

Returning to the questions posed in the second paragraph of this chapter, we can say with illumination that we are here to grow and to actualize our humanity; to learn to love. When the physical body dies, the core of our personality, commonly called the soul and the seat of our 'higher' impulses in the realm of aesthetic, moral and spiritual awareness, continues to survive and learn in a new milieu. It is well within the range of possibility that it may reincarnate in another human form, as is taught in the great religions of the East.

We cannot define with certainty the intentions of God, but those who know him through mystical experience have no doubt that his nature is pure love. In the familiar words of Julian of Norwich, 'All shall be well, and all manner of thing shall be well.'[28] Those who have behaved destructively to others will certainly suffer in the afterlife, not by being hurt by a vengeful deity but through their own isolation from the light and love of communication with their fellows, in a very different environment from that which they knew when they functioned in a physical body. But all is not lost: they too may emerge from their self-inflicted hell of isolation when they have seen the truth of their earthly behaviour and have repented with sincerity. God alone can know the intentions of the soul, but when it is ready for release into the greater light it will be received with joy. And it will know joy also. 'In love there is no room for fear; indeed perfect love banishes fear. For fear has to do with punishment, and anyone who is afraid has not attained to love in its perfection.'[29]

The proper relationship between the gifted human and their Lord is one of openness and the desire for service. 'The eye with which I see God is the same eye with which God sees me,' as Meister Eckhart said. The relationship is one of equality, a distinctly blasphemous

statement to the ardent religionist and one that landed Eckhart in a
dungeon. In fact, the religionist worships an image of God, either a
pious stereotype such as one may find in a place of worship or else an
image in their own mind. If Eckhart's opponents had known the true
God they would not have hurt him, because they would have been
imbued with love. 'God is love; he who dwells in love is dwelling in
God, and God in him.'[30]

The physical body is easily hurt because of its frailty. This is a
property of all living forms, but the human frame is especially
vulnerable. This is to teach us to take care of everything in the world
while we are alive. The fear of death that we all have, even if some
deny it, is a built-in mechanism to prevent us endangering our life in a
foolhardy way. God has given us this type of sensitive body as a means
of growing in responsibility towards life in general and working to
relieve pain in others wherever we encounter it. Until we too have
experienced suffering we cannot enter fully into life.

Upon Reflection

The innocent Christ did not suffer to quiet an angry deity, but merely
as co-operating, assisting and uniting with that love of God which
desired our salvation.

He did not suffer in our place or stead, but only on our account,
which is a quite different matter. And to say that he suffered in our
place and stead is as absurd, as contrary to Scripture, as to say that he
rose from the dead and ascended into heaven in our place and stead,
that we might be excused from it.

For his sufferings, death, resurrection and ascension are all of them
equally on our account, for our sake, for our good and benefit, but
none of them possible to be in our stead.

William Law, *The Spirit of Love*[31]

Nothing burns in hell except self-will.

The *Theologia Germanica*[32]

If you ask what is this one true, simple, plain, immediate and unerring
way, it is the way of patience, meekness, humility and resignation to
God. This is the truth and perfection of dying to self . . .

For to seek to be saved by patience, meekness, humility of heart, and
resignation to God is truly coming to God through Christ; and when
these tempers live and abide in you as the spirit and aim of your life,
then Christ is in you of a truth and the life that you lead is not yours,

but it is Christ that lives in you. For this is following Christ with all your power. You cannot possibly make more haste after Him, you have no other way of walking as He walked or depending on Him, but by wholly giving up yourself to that which He was, viz.; to patience, meekness, humility, and resignation to God.

William Law, *The Spirit of Love* [33]

5

Faith and reason: the two ways of approaching truth

> Do your utmost to support your faith with goodness, goodness with understanding, understanding with self-control ... The possession and growth of these qualities will prevent your knowledge of our Lord Jesus Christ from being ineffectual or unproductive. (2 Peter 1.5–8, *New Jerusalem Bible*)

The human mind is not a static mechanism; it is on the move constantly when we are awake. It confronts phenomena in ceaseless movement. The biblical Letter to the Hebrews, in the eleventh chapter, first defines the concept of faith and then considers the matter of faith in the past in considerable detail. 'Faith gives substance to our hopes and convinces us of realities we do not see.' Then follows the observation that people of old won God's approval for their faith. By faith, it is claimed, we understand how the world was formed at God's command, 'so that the visible came forth from the invisible'.

Then follows an inspiring précis of Hebrew history: Abel offered a greater sacrifice than Cain's and God approved his offerings and attested his goodness; likewise Enoch was taken up to another life without passing through death. 'Without faith it is impossible to please [God], for whoever comes to God must believe that he exists and rewards those who seek him.' The same train of thought accompanies the prodigies of Noah, Abraham and his descendants Isaac and Jacob; while Sarah was enabled to conceive after the menopause because she judged that God who promised would keep faith. Therefore from one man as good as dead, there sprang innumerable descendants.

All of these died in faith, for 'although they had not received the things promised, yet they had seen them far ahead and welcomed them, and acknowledged themselves to be strangers and aliens without fixed abode on earth.' They longed for 'a better country, a heavenly one', where God would be fully with them.

Returning to Abraham, the writer of the Letter to the Hebrews commemorates Abraham's obedience in being ready to sacrifice his only son Isaac, despite the promise that it was through the line of Isaac that his descendants would be traced. And so the line of faith passes through Isaac to Jacob and Esau, and through Joseph to the Israelites returning home from Egypt, when they were to bury his bones with them.

The faith of Moses was instrumental under the direction of God in leading the Israelites from Egyptian slavery to the Moabite country from which he was able to see the Promised Land but not permitted to cross over into it. This enterprise of crossing the Jordan river was reserved for his adjutant Joshua. The unknown author of Hebrews continues his meditation on his ancestors' faith, referring to the prostitute Rahab and the stories of Gideon, Barak, Samson, Jephthah, David, Samuel and the prophets.[1]

The climax of this stupendous recital is the stirring conclusion:

> With this great cloud of witnesses around us, therefore, we too must throw off every encumbrance and the sin that too readily restricts us, and run with resolution the race which lies ahead of us, our eyes fixed on Jesus, the pioneer and perfector of faith. For the sake of the joy that lay ahead of him, he endured the cross, ignoring its disgrace, and has taken his seat at the right hand of the throne of God. Think of him who submitted to such opposition from sinners; that will help you not to lose heart and grow faint. In the struggle against sin, you have not yet resisted to the point of shedding your blood. You have forgotten the exhortation which addresses you as sons: My son, do not think lightly of the Lord's discipline, or be discouraged when he corrects you; for whom the Lord loves he disciplines; he chastises every son whom he acknowledges.[2]

The writer then goes on to encourage the disciples to regard chastisement as discipline, for God is treating them as sons. He is very stern on this point: a person who escapes the discipline in which all sons share, must be illegitimate and not a true son. In this respect one cannot suppress a smile, for the old wisdom is almost criminal: 'Spare the rod and spoil the child.' In fact, the modern approach to nonviolent discipline is well advised provided an alternative method of training is employed. The denial of a usual privilege for that particular day is one answer to disobedience. But to continue turning a blind eye to it does not benefit the child, who all too soon has to confront the harsh judgement of an indifferent community.

Faith is much more comprehensive than belief; it includes action to bring one's faith to fruition. In the various examples of heroes from biblical times listed in Hebrews, each was inspired to perform a momentous deed. They actualized the inspiration, and a dramatic effect followed. In the Gospels, Jesus frequently performs healing miracles and on several occasions he tells the person who has been cured, 'Your faith has healed you.' On the other hand, the people of Nazareth, his home town, were amazed at his wisdom and miraculous powers, yet they turned against him. He said to them, 'A prophet never lacks honour, except in his home town and in his own family.' And 'he did not do many miracles there, such was their want of faith.'[3]

The action required from a person seeking healing is the enterprise to call upon the help of the individual with the gift (the 'healer', though the essential healer is God, who works through gifted individuals). Faith allows the sick person to be open to the healing power of God. In the instance of the people of Nazareth, a heavy prejudice born of jealousy rendered them unresponsive to Jesus' healing power.

Faith should not be 'blind'; on the contrary, one should have a feeling of confidence in the healer, who in turn should be able to empathize with oneself. This is true of healing generally: medical practitioners, nurses and specialized therapists are one vital component of the healing process, so also are the various types of drugs prescribed. These obviously cannot empathize, but they may impart hope and confidence in addition to their pharmacological effect. This non-physiological action is called the 'placebo effect'.

The way of reason, as opposed to the way of faith, is logical and direct. It is intellectually based, easily confirmed, and should win unanimous assent. The teaching method is necessarily based on reason, for this is the way we communicate with our fellows. Indeed, no matter how we may know the truth, whether by inspiration, psychic sensitivity, or measurement, we communicate it to others in a rational way. The scientific method is the throne of reason and its monarch is truth. It is governed by repeatable experiment by various trained investigators, or unqualified people of intelligence, who know how the world functions through their experience of life.

In this mode of reference reason stands entire; the only faith it requires is that the body and the mind are in good condition. But this is a very superficial account of the life of a human. The computer is the image of the new person: accurate, efficient and well-controlled, but lacking a sense of values apart from its program and the desire of its programmer. Its spontaneity is decidedly limited and likely to be aberrant. The emotional life of the rationalist is usually devoid of an understanding of spiritual matters. Reason, not religion, is the final court of appeal. This is somewhat ironic, for reason has little information to provide about the deep things of life and death, whereas religion is frequently so bigoted that it may conjure up fear and superstition as well as being a divisive influence in a community. This emphasizes the difference between spirituality and religion. The first is inspired by love, the second may be controlled by power. The way of the rationalist is dry, unimaginative and frequently dogmatic in its unbelief. Its contribution to human progress is limited, despite the important scientific advances that are frequently reported in the media.

One has only to look back on the twentieth century to see where rational progress has affected life on the earth. There have indeed been 'wars and rumours of wars'. We should not be alarmed, but the end is still to come. Nations and kingdoms will go to war against each other. There will be famines and earthquakes in many places, but all these things are the first birth-pangs of the new age.[4]

Every age has doubtless had some aspect of the apocalyptic vision found in the Gospel, but the twentieth century has been so brutal and destructive that the world seems to be teetering on the brink of total, irreversible collapse. But the end of Jesus' prophecy is one of hope, and this too is part of the present scene.

There is a need for faith in a new world order, inasmuch as sexual discrimination, racial prejudice and belligerence are greatly reduced in the Western European countries and much of North America. What is desperately needed is a leap of faith guided by reason, by which the prosperous nations will join ranks with the poorly developed ones. A proper sharing of resources would certainly diminish the tendency to war and civil strife throughout the world. The best way to end violence is to educate people to become deeply concerned with their own country, its development and its collaboration with its neighbours. The end might conceivably be a type of world union of which the present United Nations Organization is a reasonably sound prototype.

The secret of happiness is to lose oneself in God's business, which is the regeneration of the earth and the mending of wounded relationships. This starts on a personal basis and broadens to an interpersonal linkage. It spreads through goodwill to bind nations and various racial groups firmly in mutual respect and care. None of this is possible until faith in humanity springs up as a world phenomenon. There is no finer work than being of assistance to one's neighbours, who ultimately include all people and all that lives. When we cease to regard ourselves as special in an exclusive setting and can mix joyfully with our universal neighbour, there will be more warmth than merely a guarded peace in place of open hostility.

Faith has the confidence to put the impossible into practice at once. There is no reserve because one is working from a higher centre within oneself. This is where the inner psychic awareness lifts up the heart to the divine essence, which is the presence of God in the soul. This is how we know the Holy Spirit. At present not many people know the Spirit as a living presence, because their attention is rigidly focused on their own concerns. In such an ambience there is little opportunity for spiritual growth.

The preliminary requisite for a straight (honest, candid, not evasive) faith is clear thought and a direct confrontation with one's emotions, desires and aspirations. Nothing should be hidden from one's sight. The question arises: is one's faith true? It may be part of a great spiritual tradition or simply smooth, fundamentalistic religious teaching. The two are very different, inasmuch as the first is a representation of human aspiration to the divine, whereas the second may be merely a way of escape from the reality of the present moment to a self-satisfying world of emotional ease and comfort. A great deal of popular religion has this illusory ring to it. It is fuelled by appealing to personal indecision, theological ignorance, fear and intolerance, a constant menace to ardent piety.

If we consider the early apparitions seen by the disciples in the Acts of the Apostles, there is little doubt that they left a permanent imprint on the group, for instance their greatly enhanced confidence in times of trial. Indeed, the prerequisite for a strong faith is openness to a new possibility. Where does credulity end and intelligent trust commence? There seems to be a borderland between myth and reality. Does the phenomenon fit into a pattern of mere coincidence, or does it produce a shattering impact on the life of the person who experienced it?

Some of the criteria of judgement are:

(a) Was the apparition witnessed by other individuals?
(b) Was it repeated on a number of occasions?
(c) Did it have a positive effect in making the percipient more receptive to spiritual reality (the presence of God)?
(d) Did it broaden the percipient's sense of communal responsibility (the moral effect)?

The message of faith is transmitted psychically and spiritually. The spiritual aspect transforms the personality of the recipient, and may make them capable of deeds far beyond their previous capacity. The psychical aspect broadens the mind so that it is in contact with dimensions of reality, such as the afterlife, which are normally far outside rational experience.

Faith is our way to personal growth, but it should be checked against the deeper experience of other people of wisdom and experience, lest we lose ourselves in an enthusiasm that separates us disastrously from our peers. There is a close link between faith and grace. Necessary qualities for the burgeoning of faith are humility, clarity of thought and independence of observation. One thing is certain: a life of reason may be safe in its precision, but the way of faith never allows us to rest in certitude. The final criterion of the acceptability of a revelation is its truth and its self-evident authority.

Upon Reflection

Stillness, prayer, love and self-control are a four-horsed chariot bearing the intellect to heaven.

St Thalassios in the *Philokalia*[5]

'Many a man,' writes Hilton, 'has virtues . . . only in his reason and in his will, without any spiritual delight in them or love for them.' We may know what is right and be disposed to do it, but none the less experience 'grouchiness, depression, and bitterness' as we go about it (I, 14). In Hilton's terminology we are reformed in 'faith' but not yet in 'feeling'.

In *The Scale of Perfection* Hilton describes ways by which feelings are gradually integrated with our fundamental orientation towards God.

This 'reformation in faith and feeling' is a work of grace: humans can at most cooperate with God in it.

Julia Gatta in *A Pastoral Art* [6]

What is heaven to a reasonable soul? Nought else but Jesus God.

Walter Hilton, *The Ladder of Perfection* [7]

It is the sensibility of the soul that must receive what this world can communicate to it. It is the sensibility of the soul that must receive what God can communicate to it. Reason may follow after in either case and view through its own glass what is done, but it can do no more.

William Law, *A Demonstration of Errors* [8]

True faith is coming to Jesus Christ to be saved and delivered from a sinful nature, as the Canaanitish woman came to Him and would not be denied.

William Law, *The Grounds and Reasons* [9]

6

A loving God: with so much suffering in the world?

God is Love; he who dwells in love is dwelling in God, and God in him. This is how love has reached its perfection among us, so that we may have confidence on the day of judgement; and this we can have, because in this world we are as he is. (1 John 4.16–17)

It is indeed paradoxical, that a God of love inflicts so much pain on his human creatures. Stressing the humanity of suffering life does not overlook the pain endured by the simpler, humbler creatures who are our brethren, but merely emphasizes the acute sensitivity of the human as compared with the apparently duller feeling nature of the rest of the animal kingdom. And here there may be a lack of understanding, inasmuch as we are inevitably ignorant of the feelings of other animals. But the bareness of aesthetic creativity and the paucity of individual relationships among other animals would seem to justify this assumption. It is good indeed that cruelty to animals has been a penal offence in civilized countries for a long time, and activities on behalf of animal welfare have been flourishing rather more recently. The human is the leader of enlightened concern for the living creatures of the world, and also the instigator of the greatest cruelty and destruction against them. It seems to be a universal rule of life that all injustice that has been inflicted on others is visited wholesale on the guilty party. But what about the victim? For example, those who are murdered by an evil criminal, or the six million Jews slaughtered in the Holocaust?

In this respect it is important to separate the suffering inflicted by deranged humans from that consequent on natural disasters like earthquakes, hurricanes and floods. The latter can with reason be attributed to a flaw in the structure of the universe, perhaps due to the error or perversity of its creator, whom we honour with the name of God. In fact, even this explanation may be naïve; it is not impossible that there may be a movement of objects by mental effort without the action of physical forces. This alleged phenomenon is called psychokinesis, and is most attractive to the psychically sensitive enthusiast. Professional parapsychologists tend to be less impressed, but on occasions even they have to throw doubt aside and be more open to the possibility of this and other alleged psychical phenomena. If psychokinesis were to be proved definitely to occur, it could explain natural disasters in terms of vast psychic disturbances among large human populations, influencing the environment in which we all live. It was the custom at one time for the entire population of a country to join in prayer, after prolonged flooding or drought, that God might arrest the situation, and the result was invariably positive. Such prayer certainly appeared to have a calming effect. Whether this effect is due to the deity being moved directly with compassion, as the biblical narratives assumed with trust, or simply due to the changed mood of the population in the face of imminent disaster is a matter of opinion. This process might be a significant factor in stabilizing the weather over considerable areas. In either way, the Spirit of God (the Holy Spirit) would be active.

It seems evident that we are not meant to spend most of our life in empty enjoyment. If we were so to comport ourselves, we would grow neither as individuals nor as people. Individual growth taxes and sharpens our special abilities and also makes us keenly aware of our incapacitating deficiencies. These are as important for our maturation, which is the end point of our earthly growth, as are our glowing abilities. Community growth, in which the individuals forgo their special demands and flow into the general run of the community of which they are a part, develops their ability to fraternize with a considerable range of people. Here the individual is subsumed in the community, a far more telling achievement. In this way the individual becomes a person, one of a society of people in which all can give of themselves to others and receive accordingly. There is little place for self-glorification in such an environment, but ample opportunity for self-sacrifice.

It would not be difficult to enumerate the principal pains of life. They start at birth when the bonds of attachment are severed and the baby is free in surroundings that are cold and severe compared with

the warmth and acceptance of the abode they recently knew. The first
sound the newborn child makes is a cry; it is welcomed as a sign of a
happy birth and an earnest of what is to come. Soon the newcomer
learns that crying is no longer as welcome at the beginning of the day,
for now it disturbs the sleep of the parents and the comfortable
thoughts of those who rest themselves nearby. The life of an infant is
one of being placed firmly and deliberately into the small space
marked out for him or her. At least this space is somewhat sacrosanct
in the beginning, because it houses a new being, a little life of light
and movement. Fortunately a fundamental quality of human nature is
adaptability, and soon the infant feels secure in the worldly home,
provided the human protectors are loving and solicitous about its
welfare. This, in a small way, is the pattern of a human life, at least in
Western society, in the stages of infancy and childhood up to
adolescence in a caring family.

Adult life, at least in the early period, is influenced principally by
two considerations: the need for employment and sexual maturation
that normally culminates in marriage. The necessity of finding work is
obviously determined by economic factors, since the adult needs to be
less dependent on the help of parents and family and more able to live
comfortably alone. In the beginning, adult life may be darkened by a
degree of turmoil; past certainties are questioned, and the chilling,
major hard work of the past is harshly succeeded by even more
formidable undertakings in the future.

The experience of sexual awakening and love is associated, in
healthy young people, with irrepressible delight and activity. The
delight is best preserved by sharing it with others in living creatively
together. This is achieved by giving oneself to others in loving service,
by caring for those in desperate straits or less severe circumstances of
bodily enfeeblement like the aged or the blind. This view sees love in
its right context, memorably exalted in John 13.34–5, and John
15.12–17, which is a joyful giving of itself for the benefit of the other
person or animal. Unless sexual intercourse takes place in this spirit,
the operative energy is physical lust, not emotional, let alone spiritual,
love.

The great ideal of early adult life is success, whether financial,
sexual or social. There is an increasing reliance on the help of friends
and colleagues, and a warmth of affection should lift the association
above mere convenience to a concern which may burgeon into
spontaneous love. Love knows no genital barriers and should be as

strong towards one's own sex as to the other. How it is expressed is a
private matter between the two people, but it should be done in good
order, as applies to private undertakings in general.

Social success is usually a combination of sexual satisfaction and
financial achievement, and its end is a pleasant home with a married
partner and family. But a gay establishment is not in any way to be
belittled. What matters in all personal relationships is the commitment between the partners and the love that flows from it. It would
not be too extreme to say that the ultimate measure of a person's life is
the magnitude of their contribution to society; this may be an
impressive list of achievements in the arts or sciences or simply a mere
giving of oneself to others.

Financial success is always pleasant, no matter what political creed
one espouses. And it is good that the young person goes all-out in the
pursuit of material and sexual satisfaction; the 'sowing of one's wild
oats' is necessary for the vigorous type of person who needs to feel the
full force of their life-energy at its peak before more serious issues arise
to divert them to darker themes. We all learn by experience, and the
type of experience we need seems to be the one invariably meted out
to us. It is in the vantage point between suffering and relief that we
may survey the course of our past life, assessing both its inadequacies
and its possibilities, and making some inner commitments about what
we believe to be the truth. From this may emerge a definite decision
about our future endeavours.

On the surface, in our society a successful adult life is usually
measured in terms of career satisfaction as well as financial stability
and social status. Indeed, quite a few solid citizens can display
material success and an impressive home with many fine paintings as
well as smaller objets d'art. Likewise, their family will have all it
desires.

In due course, misfortune strikes the superficially happy house-
hold. This is at present, as it has always been in the past, an invariable
part of life. Suffering is the centre of life. To some it comes early on,
to others towards the end, and not a few are born in pain – in which
instance the suffering is very likely to be inflicted by a deranged parent
or nurse. Some mentally disturbed people enjoy inflicting pain on
defenceless humans or animals. But why do these monsters bear their
fearful whip?

The usual causes of suffering are physical and mental ill-health, a
broken relationship which may follow the death of a beloved parent,

sibling or long-established partner, or a severe disappointment in a career that had all the promise of joyful fulfilment. This fulfilment is more than mere financial success; it could have creative overtones in music, writing or painting or in counselling or spiritual direction. The feature all the above misfortunes have in common is the comparatively sudden and irreversible blow that they strike, so that in one way or another the life of the person is at least temporarily shattered. But why? The great majority of victims throughout the ages have not been notoriously evil people. Indeed, quite a few heroes have emerged from their midst. In this respect we can consider the victims of the Nazi death camps of the twentieth century. Where was a God of love in all this?

A little light is shed on this mystery of apparently undeserved suffering in the Book of Job, a great literary masterpiece of the Old Testament. Here we consider a perfectly just man, Job, who cares greatly for the poor and rejected of society, yet is suddenly laid low by a series of devastating misfortunes that destroy all his wealth, his family, and finally his health also. Three friends come to commiserate with him, but the comfort they offer is superficial, and the explanations they suggest as the cause of his misfortune are commonplace and unhelpful. In the end he lays his complaint directly before God, and after a fourth speaker makes his appearance and adds little to the argument, God himself interposes. He points out how feeble and ignorant Job is compared with the deity. Job is duly repentant to have challenged the Creator, and at last goes home to encounter a new restoration, including a quite different family.

Commentators have suggested that Job's special sin was to have magnified his own righteousness before his friends and God also, as is evidenced in his speeches of self-justification in chapters 29 to 31 (which precede Elihu's, the fourth speaker's, interposition in chapters 32 to 37). This is the only criticism one can lay at the door of Job – if indeed one is heartless enough to blame a person in such terrible straits for any undisciplined thought at all.

It is generally agreed that the 'happy ending' of the Book of Job was written as an addendum by another contributor later on, because the style is different from that of the rest of the book. Be that as it may, the principle is firm: no one can escape the inroads of misfortune in the course of one's life, but the person who is courageous will prevail, and experience a far deeper blessing. But what about the instances of the innocent who are wantonly assaulted and die soon afterwards – to say nothing of the millions who have been savagely murdered as victims of the waves of genocide that have defaced the outwardly ultracivilized twentieth century?

The solution of this apparently unanswerable problem is found, as far as it can be found, in the writings of the New Testament. Here the life of the world to come is unambiguously proclaimed and the value of a life given over to Christ's service assured.[1] However, this service is to be measured as a devoted act of love for all humanity whatever religion it may profess, remembering that the name of Christ itself can be used as a catchphrase to justify such actions as the Crusades, the Spanish Inquisition, and the vicious persecution of the Jews for the past two millennia, including the Holocaust of the twentieth century.

As we read in the Sermon on the Mount:

> Not everyone who says to me, 'Lord, Lord' will enter the kingdom of Heaven, but only those who do the will of my heavenly Father. When the day comes, many will say to me, 'Lord, Lord, did we not prophesy in your name, drive out demons in your name, and in your name perform many miracles?' Then I will tell them plainly, 'I never knew you. Out of my sight; your deeds are evil!'[2]

Incidentally, this quotation indicates that spiritual gifts are not invariably of divine nature, a far cry from the fruits, or harvest, of the Holy Spirit, which are blessed manifestations of the love of God that always tend to glorify those on whom they alight and from whom they pour down. We have considered this matter in chapter 3.

Upon Reflection

Ponder these meditations from the fourteenth-century mystic Julian of Norwich, in her *Revelations of Divine Love*:

> I saw no anger except on man's side, and He forgives that in us, for anger is nothing else but a perversity and an opposition to peace and to love. And it comes from a lack of power, or a lack of wisdom, or a lack of goodness, and this lack is not in God, but is on our side.[3]

> All our travail is because love is lacking on our side.[4]

> And so I saw most surely that it is quicker for us and easier to come to the knowledge of God than it is to know our own soul.[5]

> Sin is necessary but all will be well, and all will be well, and every kind

of thing will be well. In this naked world I was compelled to admit that everything which is done is well done, for our Lord God does everything.[6]

The reason which we use is now so blind, so abject and so stupid that we cannot recognize God's exalted, wonderful wisdom, or the power and the goodness of the blessed Trinity. And this is his intention when he says: You will see yourself that every kind of thing will be well.[7]

For he regards sin as sorrow and pain for his lovers, to whom for love he assigns no blame.[8]

Man is changeable in this life, and falls into sin through naiveté and ignorance. He is weak and foolish in himself, and also his will is overpowered in the time when he is assailed and in sorrow and woe. And the cause is blindness, because he does not see God, for if he saw God continually, he would have no harmful feelings nor any kind of prompting, no sorrowing which is conducive to sin.[9]

No more than his love towards us is withdrawn because of our sin, does he wish our love to be withdrawn from ourselves or from our fellow Christians.[10]

7

A sacramental way: seeing holiness in everything

Teach me, my God and King
In all things Thee to see,
And what I do in any thing
To do it as for Thee.

(George Herbert)

Inasmuch as everything ultimately comes from God, so that whatever we may give to other creatures has a divine origin, we are fundamentally mere transmitters of universal holiness. But how easily the divine nature can be soiled, polluted and even perverted by sinful humans working in collaboration with the forces of nature all around them! What do we want most of all in life? Various thoughts come to us as we confront this testing question.

The first observation that may enter our mind is a sorry remembrance of the appalling human suffering that disfigured the whole of the twentieth century: two world wars with all the destructive potential of modern conflict, genocidal murder of millions of fellow humans motivated by racial, religious and national hatred, and natural disasters due to earthquakes, floods and cyclones. The news broadcast daily on television keeps us all up to date with the horror of so much of contemporary life, and the more cynical of us dismiss the very suggestion that there is any organizing power in the world. Or if there is, that power is careless and scarcely moral, despite the assertions of the higher religions about the love of God. What most people want most of all in their life is physical safety, which may be expanded to care in an unfriendly environment.

Many people yearn for more money; they believe that ultimate satisfaction is attained by material security, to the point of excess. A grasping nature is always at war with someone else and not infrequently with many others. The more we share, the more we can expand in the depth of our being. The more we conceal, the more we contract inwardly, to guard our precious possessions from possible interference from an outside source. Jesus asked, 'What will anyone gain by winning the whole world at the cost of his life? Or what can he give to buy his life back?'[1]

If we were to analyse our most immediately pertinent desire, it would surely be for love and security. But this is barely compatible with a grasping nature. While we are at war with ourselves we cannot accommodate love, and our internal unease makes security a distant hope only. If we take our religious commitment seriously, we have to get our priorities in order, by putting God first through the practice of prayer.

The essence of prayer is a deep silence in the soul, that aspect of the personality where attitudes of morality issue forth as spontaneously as the movements of breathing and the tendency to focus the mind moment by moment. When we have entered this silence as happily as we might have done at some previous period when the mind was flooded with ideas and we were aiming at some idealistic goal, we know we are still before a mighty presence, and can listen with an acute sensitivity to its enunciation of the truth of our spiritual state.

God comes to us by his grace. We cannot bring him to our assistance by loud cries, any more than by imperious commands, but somehow he is at our side when we need him. The secret is, of course, that he is always at hand as our universal protector and friend, but our awareness of his presence is dulled by our own selfish desires and despairing fears. As soon as we strive to be quiet, a psychic feeler seems to extrude from ourself to the source of all life, which is one way of addressing God, and a deeper awareness of strength and peace flows into us. The words of prayer are useful if they are said with earnest intent, but the deepest prayer can be completely wordless, even in silent conversation to an unseen, unheard source. If prayer is to be valid it should be sustained through the long watches of the night, so that its impact remains with us in the busy, diverting day also. In other words, do not stop praying.

Prayer as a category of worship in a well-rehearsed liturgy (a form of public worship) can easily, through constant repetition, become merely a series of sentences and phrases enunciated by rote. 'Saying one's prayers' can be a stereotyped recital to the extent that one does not pay sufficient attention to the words. The correct response to the direction, 'let us pray', is silence and a reaching within to the depths of one's being (the soul) where one knows stillness and peace. This sounds simple enough, but it may require a lifetime's experience of pain and disappointment to attain. Self-assertiveness is incompatible with prayer, because one's attention is fixed primarily on oneself and not on God or other people. Prayer is a lifting up of the mind to God, not by thought but by ardent love. This love opens the soul to the full presence of divine love.

The person who lives in the sacramental way is open to divine communication at all times. This is clearly the way of the saint, and it should be striven for by us all. With it comes a keen compassion for one's fellows, which shows itself progressively in a concern for animals and vegetation also. It is possible to strive for sanctity, just as one's less enlightened peers will hanker after the good things of life like wealth, popularity or power. The person who really desires a reputation for saintliness will certainly be subjected to pain and distress. This is not to be seen as a punishment by an angry God out to teach the self-appointed initiate to think less highly of himself, or herself. It is an inevitable consequence of exposing oneself to the various deleterious elements that vitiate the psychic atmosphere where one lives one's inner life. One can be overwhelmed by the malice of the forces in this realm, so that one may be tempted to give up.

The forces of darkness native to the psychic world emanate from both the living and the deceased. They include fear, hatred, jealousy, destructiveness and dishonesty. We all know how sapping of one's strength these negative influences can be even when the world seems to be in good order; when circumstances are in a mess, the forces of darkness may be greatly magnified in power, and the way forward is by silent prayer. What we cannot affect directly on the psychic-emotional plane, is open to spiritual intervention. If the source of the trouble is a living person, then it is necessary to overhaul the relationship in order to discover what exactly is wrong and to rectify matters accordingly. If a discarnate entity (popularly called a 'spirit') is responsible for the trouble, the way forward is by means of prayer in which the entity is lifted up to God. Occasionally a ministry of deliverance (exorcism) may be necessary, but this should be under-taken only by a specialist in the field, who should be ordained, for the entity may on occasion be extremely malevolent. The essential requirement in the work of deliverance is love. The teaching of Jesus is clear: 'Do not resist those who wrong you. If anyone slaps you on the right cheek, turn and offer him the other also.'[2]

It may be objected quite reasonably that the teaching in the Sermon on the Mount[3] is impractical for the world we are obliged to inhabit. How can we love what is frankly evil? Jesus would say that things which are completely impossible for mortals are well within God's compass.[4] Therefore by all means choose your company with care, but do not reject anyone categorically. That person (or angel) is also a child of God, no matter how far they may have fallen from grace. It is one thing to show one's displeasure unequivocally but another to seek to destroy something in disgust or fear.

The forces of darkness peculiar to any one individual are not essentially different from those mentioned above, but they afflict the person from the time of birth. They make an indelible mark on the person's character, that collection of qualities or characteristics, especially of a mental or moral nature, that are distinctive for an individual. Dealing with the grossest character defects is the preserve of the psychotherapist, but minor weaknesses can be dealt with by the individual person, once that person is made aware of the trouble. This may, for example, be a tendency to look down on people of a different background, to envy those who appear to be more fortunate than oneself, to spread scandal or fear, or to lack self-respect or self-confidence. It is doubtful whether anyone besides the great saints of humanity has a completely inviolate character.

Life is our great moral teacher. Meditating on the lives of the apostles is a lesson in saintly growth: from a group of cowards who denied so much as knowing their Master when he was in greatest need, they were able to confront their own despicable behaviour and eat the dust of humiliation. They were then forgiven by Christ and were able to form the earliest Christian congregation. It is noteworthy that the one apostle who separated himself from the others was Judas Iscariot, who is portrayed as the traitor leading armed men to seize Jesus.[5] He subsequently hanged himself.[6] A more spectacular account of the death of Judas Iscariot is described in Acts 1.18: he 'fell headlong and burst open so that all his entrails spilled out'. Whatever may be the truth, it seems evident that Judas did not seek forgiveness like the other eleven apostles.

To live in a sacramental way one's awareness should always be focused on God. This does not mean thinking of God continuously –

if one were to proceed thus there would be no opportunity for doing one's work in the world, which might demand times of rapt attention. If one's awareness is centred on God, he is one's friend and guide at all times. This blessed state of divine awareness is the precious fruit of unfailing contemplative prayer. This is how St Paul's command to 'pray without ceasing'[7] is obeyed. In this state of contemplation there is a continuous background of divine love which supports the full mental life of the individual. When one knows the sacramental way one can never be lonely, because a sense of caring is always with one.

The corollary of the sacramental life is a deep caring for all and sundry. No one is a stranger any longer, and one's life is devoted to the needs of the entire community. The finest inspirations we have at hand are the world's religious geniuses, of whom Jesus is the most universal example. A study of the Gospels is most inspiring in this respect. The shortest of these, that of St Mark, is particularly valuable because it provides a dynamic account of Jesus' actions with a considerably shortened teaching section.

The proof of a person's deep love for God is one's love of the world, primarily of one's fellow creatures. This is the essence of a sacrament – a religious ceremony or act of the Christian churches regarded as an outward and visible sign of inward and spiritual grace. By grace is meant a freely given, undeserved gift from God. In the Eastern and Roman Catholic churches there are seven sacraments (baptism, confirmation, the Eucharist, matrimony, penance, extreme unction and ordination), whereas in most Protestant denominations these are restricted to baptism and the Eucharist.

It is noteworthy that the Christian group with by far the finest reputation for non-violence and social enlightenment, the Society of Friends (or Quakers), do not have sacraments at all in their weekly silent time of an hour's prayer together. But this does not imply a rejection of specific sacraments. It simply indicates that the committed Quaker regards all life as sacramental, a necessary development of the insight stated by George Fox, the founder of the denomination, that 'there is that of God in every man'.

This is indeed the sacramental way, and anyone who lives it faithfully will see Christ in their neighbour, just as Jesus revealed himself to the two travellers on the melancholy journey to Emmaus described in Luke 24 (see above, chapter 2).

Upon Reflection

The place of religion is within; its work and effect is within; its glory, its life, its perfection is all within; it is merely and solely the raising of a new life, a new love, and a new birth in the inward spirit of our hearts.

William Law, *The Spirit of Prayer*[8]

Teach us O God that silent language which says all things. Teach our souls to remain silent in thy presence that we may adore Thee in the deeps of our being and await all things from Thee whilst asking of Thee nothing but the accomplishment of thy will. Teach us to remain quiet under thine action and produce in our souls that deep and simple prayer which says nothing and expresses everything, which specifies nothing and expresses everything.

Père Grou (1731–1803)[9]

Grace is given to attract and draw the soul into the rest of love, and not into the many ways of the self ...

The interior is not a stronghold to be taken by storm and violence; but a kingdom of peace, which is to be gained only by love.

Madame Guyon (1648–1717), *A Short and Easy Method of Prayer*[10]

Let us learn the wonder of this sacrament, the purpose of its institution, the effects it produces. We become a single body, according to Scripture, members of his flesh and bone of his bones. This is what is brought about by the food that he gives us. He blends himself with us so that we may all become one single entity in the way the body is joined to the head.

John Chrysostom (fourth century), *Homily on John* 46[11]

Men, women, children, deeply divided as to race, nationality, language, class, work, knowledge, rank and fortune ... are all created afresh by the Church in the Spirit. On all alike she impresses a divine form. All receive from her a unique unbreakable nature, a nature that does not allow any account to be taken henceforward of the manifold and deep differences which distinguish them. Thereby all are united in a truly catholic way. In the Church no one is in any way separated from the community. Everyone is, so to speak, merged into everyone else, by the simple and indivisible power of faith ... Christ is thus everything in everyone, Christ who incorporates everything in himself in accordance with the infinite and all-wise power of his goodness. He is the centre upon which all lines converge so that the creatures of the one God may not remain strangers or enemies to one another for lack of common ground on which to display their friendliness and their peace.

Maximus the Confessor (*c*. 580–662), *Mystagogia*[12]

Then take the towel, and break the bread,
and humble us, and call us friends;
suffer and serve till all are fed
and show how grandly love intends
to work till all creation sings,
to fill all worlds, to crown all things.

Brian Wren[13]

8

False gods and human crutches: the power of illusion in life

The best way to learn about the love of God is to love him. (Madame Guyon)

A god may be regarded as a superhuman being or spirit worshipped as having power over nature, human fortune and the general flow of life; a deity in the form of an image or idol worshipped as divine or symbolized as a god. This is an age-old illusion, and forms the basis of the various charms carried by people in the course of their daily life. They feel reassured by having such an omen of good fortune close to them, and the power of suggestion may play its part in keeping up their spirits during times of great stress.

This is a far cry from the God (or deity) of Christianity and other monotheistic religions, who is worshipped as the supreme being and Creator and ruler of the universe. The one true God brings a person's whole life into balance; fear and superstition are shed, irrational dread of the unknown or unexplained is much lessened, and the personality can pause in strength to face a new experience in trust and with warmth of heart.

Life is indeed a mysterious process: the medical basis is remarkably well understood but the mental concomitant is less well defined. This takes us to the psychic realm, which is a complete mystery to most people, especially the intellectually arrogant who base all psychic phenomena on a rationalistic level. These phenomena are described by the 'sensitive' as messages or other forms of communication that are transmitted spontaneously to them in the absence of a sensory source.

Those communications that come spontaneously have a strongly emotional charge. They may be useful in revealing to the sensitive an aspect of their character or even their future, whereas any message that is conveyed by someone else should in the great majority of instances be treated with reserve. Psychic communication and mediumship, except in the hands of exceptionally able, dedicated people, is a minefield of illusion, and should not be sought except for parapsychological research.

Mediumistic communication with the deceased is strictly forbidden in the Bible, and with good reason.[1] Fraud, whether by a medium or by a discarnate communicator, is too common to make the practice in any way reliable, and there is also the danger of becoming contaminated by a demonic agent. But it may happen on an unexpected occasion that a bereaved person feels convinced that the deceased party is communicating with them. They should then be left unhindered to decide whether this is true or illusory.

Most of the false gods that humanity seeks are distinctly human. Eminent people form one distinguished group. They may wield power which makes them a centre of attraction. Political parties may assume a godlike character by virtue of the policies their adherents espouse. Political activity is meat and drink to some individuals; its appeal may slacken somewhat with age, but this is by no means invariable. The same attitude may apply to the almost godlike reputation of some celebrated people, whether in politics or some other walk of life.

Some people are justly called luminaries, inasmuch as they are sources of intellectual light or moral inspiration. They play an intermediate role in our spiritual life, for though they are not divine, they indicate something of the way to God by their very presence as well as by the nature of their life. The saints of various religions come into this category, but no matter how greatly we may esteem them, we are wise not to confuse them with the deity. It is, though, quite in order to pray *through* them, seeing them as points of contact with God. Praying *to* them is a more questionable practice because it can easily proceed to superstitious reliance, whereas in fact our help is in the Lord alone.

The society with which we identify ourselves can quite easily assume the proportions of a god. We measure ourselves with sure confidence against different nations and races; this tendency proceeds insidiously in the direction of nationalism and racism to the extent that a person's accent, appearance or general attitude becomes an attractive feature or a focus of repulsion. A false god brings with it a feeling of confidence consequent on belonging to the 'right' country, class or society. The more false the god, the more perverted is the manner of worship it induces. It is a general rule that worshippers at the shrine of a false god become increasingly inflated by their own enthusiasm, and see themselves as a relative of the god. In fact, they tend to take over the divine function. They may separate themselves and their family from what they see as a dangerous source of error; alternatively they may set out with impatient dedication to convert everyone to worshipping their own saviour.

All that has been described above is an account of a fanatical believer in thrall to an outside influence; it may be an ideology or a person with charismatic powers. Many dictators who marred the twentieth century came into this category. It is evident that the typical false god can wield considerable power, which may well be of a psychic nature. Some of this may be contributed by the devotees themselves. False gods come easily into the category of addictions. Just as some drugs lead to such dependence that a person can only be weaned off them with considerable difficulty, so the false god takes control of the individual's inner life so radically that that person's freedom of choice is abolished. A false god tends to release the individual from responsibility – he or she has merely to turn to it to obtain reassurance and relief.

It would in fact not be too much of an exaggeration to include alcohol and habit-forming drugs in the category of universal false gods. They dominate a person's way of life so as to become the central focus around which all other events revolve. The character of a false god, whether a person or a drug, has a common feature: it clings on to a personal weakness. This is its mode of initial contact, and it then adheres to the person so that it eventually becomes a necessity for their very existence. And yet it contributes nothing in return to the welfare of its victim. This stricture would apply even to the type of drug mentioned, inasmuch as the possible immediate benefit would soon be overshadowed by the problem of dependence. It is evident that a doctor prescribing a drug should be aware of its liability to lead to addiction in relation to the length of time anticipated for the drug's use in a particular patient. The principle may usefully be extended to rituals of quite a few varieties that are unrelated to drugs and dietary habits, for example worshipping at exclusive shrines or attending various spiritual teachers' 'workshops' (meetings for concerted discussion or activity).

Dependencies of the types that have been mentioned above are not only false gods but also human crutches. Just as a pair of crutches is necessary for a person who has injured their legs so that walking would be painful, hazardous or frankly impossible due to pain or immobility, so a false god may be useful or even necessary when a person has been deprived of their dignity or hope because of a misfortune or humiliation. To claim the friendship (even if it were in truth merely an acquaintanceship) of a socially significant person in the field of politics, entertainment or religion can be a fillip to one's shattered morale. To know that one is still remembered with solicitude by people who really 'count' for something in the greater world of affairs can certainly mobilize one's self-respect. In due course these noteworthy individuals retire and become distant memories, confirming how illusory their godhead is – even if they are fine people fully deserving respect and fond remembrance. Name-dropping is a distinctly different device: it is simply using famous people whom one might have met to enhance one's own reputation. It has nothing to recommend it; it reminds one of people who try to insinuate themselves into a long queue of customers awaiting attention. The net result is irritation and derision.

When one considers the concept of a god in a clearly religious context, the main feature that stands out is the transcendent nature of the deity. In the present climate of opinion, atheism is prevalent in large sections of society. This is ultimately a great loss, but the acceptance of a divine principle which is personalized as the Supreme Creator can be used by unscrupulous adventurers and gullible fundamentalists as a means of dominating the community.

It requires a considerable intellect to confront the Entirely Other who is closer to one than one's own soul. If one can make this leap of faith, one's own imagination is vastly broadened, and one can empathize with a large range of living beings. In fact even this demand is inappropriate because the person's part in the process is purely receptive. To the mystic, God is known by the effect the encounter has in expanding their consciousness into regions of transcendental spendour. There is inexpressible joy with overflowing love and forgiveness to the creatures of the world collectively as well as individually.

This is an overwhelming experience of God, and may be defined as grace, the supernatural assistance of God bestowed on a rational being with a view to his or her sanctification. The necessity of this aid is fully acknowledged, but the manner of its action has been a subject of discussion among Christians since at least the fourth century AD. In fact, the concept is present in the prophetic writings in the Old Testament at the time of the exile to Babylon in the sixth century BC. The prophets of the exile taught that God would grant his people the ability to do his will.[2] This ability is neither earned, for instance by piety, nor deserved through good works. But when the Spirit of God (the Holy Spirit) touches our apparently insignificant person, who then wakes up (a favourite biblical analogy), our soul is set on fire and our life enters a completely new phase.

Not all of us are mystics of the intensity described above, but the important quality of a truly spiritual person is their ability to live in awareness of the present moment, which includes the work they are doing and the needs of the world at the same time. Thus they can perform their daily work well but not selfishly. Life itself becomes more exciting, not so much in terms of material reward, but rather through participation in the needs of the world. The essential means of helping is always prayer. From this practice one may be inspired to help in other ways also (but one should always beware of meddling in other people's problems uninvited). This concern is possibly the greatest joy of the spiritual life. Certainly the satisfaction that may come from it may be a light in one's own pilgrimage.

This is the way of serving the true and only God. The inspiration is not transient or even fleeting as in the case of dependence on a false god. There is no need for a material crutch, whether human or chemical. Inspired by the divine presence, strength surges through the person's mind and body, and they become capable of remarkable feats of spiritual devotion. We all have to learn that the key to a fully realized life is using our gifts and talents to their best advantage. This obviously entails much work and perseverance, but unless we are lightened by the divine spark within us, the going is liable to become extremely hard and the outcome precarious to say the least.

A false god is comparable to a flickering candle – useful in an emergency when there is a power failure and we are plunged into darkness, but its lifespan is severely limited. The one true God by contrast never comes to an end. He is transcendent of time and space. St Paul writes that love will never come to an end.[3] This love is a divine property which is the energy on which all life depends, and is the basis of our hope that our own essence, the soul, will continue to live when the accompanying body dies.

The role of religion in defining the one true God is ambivalent. It should be devoted to the worship and service of God and be the means of leading the people to him (in the monotheistic faiths), or to the Ultimate Good (in such a non-theistic faith as Buddhism). Unfortunately the paraphernalia of the faith, especially the officiating clergy (using the term in a collective manner to include all the world faiths), tend to dominate proceedings to the extent that God is in effect strongly identified with a particular religion. In this way the one true God can appear to be the sole possession of a particular religious group. The end result will be worshipping a religion rather than God, who becomes a convenient power symbol for an aggressive group of ambitious people. No faith is free from this perversion, but the worst examples are seen among the monotheistic group.

It therefore comes about with a sense of irony that religion, which is the ultimate work of humanity because it should lead us from base selfishness to a nobility of endeavour and action seen in the saints of all the great faiths, is also from time to time shot through with a false god who may completely conceal the presence of the Almighty One whom we call God.

Upon Reflection

Prayer is the application of the heart to God, and the internal exercise of love ...

Teach man to seek God in his heart, to think of him, to return to him whenever he finds he has wandered away from him, and to do and to suffer all things with the single purpose of pleasing him. This is the right way to make progress in your spiritual life. It leads the soul to the very source of God's grace. Teach people about the prayer of the heart, not of the mind; the prayer that comes from God's Spirit, not the prayer that is drawn from man's mind.

Madame Guyon, *A Short and Easy Method of Prayer*[4]

Every man that has any feeling of his sin, or any true desire to be delivered from it by Christ has learning enough to make his own prayer. For praying is not speaking forth eloquently, but simply, the true desire of the heart.

The most simple souls that have accustomed themselves to speak their own desires and wants to God, in such short but true breathings of their hearts to him, will soon know more of prayer and the mysteries of it than any who have only their knowledge from learning and learned books.

It is not silence, or a simple petition, or a great variety of outward expressions that alters the nature of prayer, or makes it good or better, but only and solely the reality, steadiness and continuity of the desire; and therefore whether a man offers this desire to God in the silent longing of the heart, or in simple short petitions, or in a great variety of words is of no consequence. But if you would know what I would call a true and great gift of prayer, and what I most of all wish for myself, it is a good heart that stands continually inclined towards God.

William Law, *The Spirit of Prayer* [5]

9

The company we keep: what we do with our thoughts and feelings

It is not our occupations that tire us out, but our pre-occupations.
(Henri Nouwen)

We each have a unique personality which, if properly used, could contribute richly to the community. We tend to envy individuals more gifted than ourselves and feel inferior to them. In this simple example there are two feelings, of envy and self-deprecation, that may be carried around in our personality. Usually these negative feelings are soon shed in the rich tapestry of life, as we see how fortunate we are compared with many other people. We may, on the other hand, have a tendency to exult in our background, our intellect or our appearance, to name only a few positive features, and our personality expands in pride. These feelings are unlikely to be shed as rapidly as simple feelings of inferiority, because we hang on to them very possessively. They are part of our treasured identity and preserve our sense of importance.

The human mind is a veritable kaleidoscope of changing thoughts and emotions. This fluctuation is governed by the state of the outside world and the health of our body. If we live permanently in this state, we have little on which to rely for permanence. Our emotional background does serve to anchor us to the present, even when it is composed of negative feelings based on past memories or current fears and irritations. If the feelings are positive, especially if wealth and power are involved, our emotional background will fix our attention firmly on our own present welfare, and we may become pleasantly self-centred. No wonder Jesus taught that it was easier for a camel to pass through the eye of a needle than for a rich man to enter the kingdom of God.[1]

Though this stricture applied to wealth, it could be said equally of any quality that might place the individual in such an advantageous position that it separates them from their fellows. If one has a remarkable gift or talent, one should share it with other people spontaneously and with love. If one clings to it selfishly, it eventually becomes one's master, even to the extent of being a false god. Our thoughts and feelings are extremely valuable in leading us to actualize our personality.

For instance, circumstances may introduce us to music when our background had no cognizance of the art. But when its beauty touches our soul, a new dimension of emotional awareness may overwhelm us and lead us to God. From this example we can see that our thoughts and feelings need not be a comfortable terminus only, but may also be the means of entering the transcendent realm where the divine is known. Our thoughts guide us to various actions and supervise their performance, but their purpose may have a moral component.

The important quality that governs their influence in our lives is awareness. As soon as we are aware of the present moment we are automatically detached from thoughts and feelings apart from that moment. It is then possible, if we retain that detachment, to view our life with its thoughts and feelings quite dispassionately. We may then distinguish between thought processes that are positive and those that are negative. Negative attitudes (ways of thinking and feeling) have their place in our spiritual life by cutting us down to size, but then our spirit should rise once more, and with a more mature outlook on life. 'When I was a child I spoke like a child, thought like a child, reasoned like a child; but when I grew up I finished with childish things.'[2]

Conversely, positive attitudes, though obviously beneficial, have their limitations also. They lift us up by giving us courage to perform deeds far beyond our customary competence. But they may increase our self-esteem to inflated heights, and alienate friends and colleagues in the process. The ideal situation is calm confidence and availability to assist others who are in trouble. As soon as we feel special in any way other than our individual identity we start to strain our connection with our fellows. Before the process leads to isolation, we are likely to experience a misfortune which leads to a strongly negative attitude. This puts us firmly in our place.

Life is essentially a learning process, and its great endeavour is to fashion substantial adults from the tiny infants that were born not so long before. Of course, much life is not of human origin, and it too has its own destiny to fulfil. If we live in calm awareness we will not only be more efficient in our daily work, but also more helpful in whatever situation we may be placed. The fact is that much thinking is desultory and a way of evading serious issues which one would rather not face directly. A truly spiritual person acquires the ability to focus their mind on the silence which is the background of God's presence. In this silence God's love reaches us directly, for it is the presence 'in whom we live and move, and in whom we exist'.[3] In that silence we experience the assurance that all is fundamentally well despite the violence that explodes from unstable people.

If we are unable to work constructively with our thoughts and feelings, they will manifest themselves destructively when circumstances are favourable for such an outburst. It is evident therefore that we should endeavour to control them by a life of quiet service and dedicated prayer. This is complicated by the thoughts of others impinging upon us. These may come from people who are hostile to us or, worse still, from evil political sources or dogmatic religious groups. This is decidedly not the company we should normally keep, or we may become indoctrinated by enthusiastic partisans, especially if our own security is endangered. These may, in addition, activate our own thoughts and feelings in a destructive manner – all perhaps in the name of the common good, or even of God! Crimes committed in the name of God continue unabated in some higher religions.

One is suspicious of religious groups that practise proselytism on a large scale; one feels that their motive is power rather than holiness. The early Christian converts could expect persecution and even death. When Christianity became an imperial religion the boot was on the other foot, and it was virtually mandatory to subscribe to the Faith. The outcome was satisfactory neither to Christianity nor to the convert, and terrible outrages were committed in the name of Christ. Such enthusiasm began to slacken at the time of the Renaissance and more radically with the Enlightenment. At present, religious observance is slack in most Western countries, but the general interest in spiritual matters is strong.

The proof of faith properly assimilated is obedience – but what sort of obedience? Is it power-driven or life-affirming? One perverse deviation is fundamentalism, the strict maintenance of ancient doctrines of any religion. There is a notable growth of fundamentalist religion in some highly successful churches at the present time, but the congregation may be so convinced that it possesses the truth that it tends to ignore deeper issues of experience. It is also highly judgemental of people whose style of life differs from their own. Jesus said, 'Do not judge, and you will not be judged.'[4] Like much other teaching in the Sermon on the Mount, this must be taken in its proper context. Of course criminal and antisocial activity must be judged and punished appropriately, but private actions that do not harm anybody else are not the concern of others. The criminal code should be our moral guideline.

The fruit of a spiritual faith is its tendency to promote growth. There should be a firm confidence in one's abilities and judgement. This confidence works in harmony with other people; it is receptive to other opinions according to its own judgement, but also accepts its own limitations as well as its own strengths. Specific negative and positive feelings fade into the background of a well-balanced personality.

Superstition, an irrational fear of the unknown or the mysterious, lessens, not so much through greater knowledge but as a result of a well-informed faith that 'all things work together for good for those who love God'.[5] It is this type of faith that is spoilt by a fundamentalist type of religion, which is desperately afraid of the devil and all his works. These works are in practice all the things of which the believer disapproves. One great biblical text seems to have escaped the fundamentalist: 'In love there is no room for fear; indeed perfect love banishes fear.'[6]

As one grows spiritually so one attains mastery of one's particular discipline. One also grows in patience, in care for others, in warmth of relationships and in concern for the wider world. At least as important as any of these is more leave to care for oneself. The more patient we are, the greater are the resources of awareness and discipline at our disposal. Socially, we become more relaxed. We can enjoy the present moment more completely, and also the presence and company of other people. We feel love more fully, remembering that 'there is no greater love than this, that someone should lay down their life for their friends'.[7]

It is evident that spiritual awareness is the only effective way of dealing with our thoughts and feelings, for then they are lifted up to God. The way to achieve this elevation is silent prayer. There are various methods of attaining inner silence. A well-tried method is simply letting one's consciousness rest on a part of the body. The navel, the heart or the top of the head are three well-known points of entry into silence. If the person can remain still in this position, an opening to a greater silence will occur. Words become superfluous, if not distracting.

What part does public worship play in our approach to God? In theory, it should concentrate the mind on higher realities, and the Eucharist should bring the worshipper to the divine presence. In practice, the action of the celebrant and the depth of prayer among the communicants are of great importance in making the sacrament meaningful to the congregation, even though the grace of God is independent of human aid. Jesus promised that where two or three people meet together in his name, he is there among them.[8] The instruction 'in his name' is most important, for it means to adopt his nature. It is easy enough to become a denominational Christian, but this is a mere title until one has opened one's heart to Christ. A true disciple follows the way shown by Christ, the main quality of which is love. The person who carries out the demands of Jesus in his or her life is a disciple, even if they have never heard his name.

Upon Reflection

I find in you anxieties, vain fears, dejection, weariness and discouragement that are half deliberate, or at least not sufficiently resisted, and that constantly disturb in you that interior peace upon the need for which I have been insisting. What are you to do to prevent them?

First, never cling to them voluntarily; secondly, neither endure nor resist them with violent effort since that merely strengthens them. Allow them to drop as a stone drops into water; think of other things; as St Francis de Sales says, talk to God of other things; take shelter in your refuge – the interior silence of respect and submission, of trust and complete self-abandonment.

How am I to behave, you may ask, if whether in this connection or in others, I commit faults, even voluntary faults? On such occasions you must recollect the counsel of St Francis de Sales: neither be troubled that you are troubled, nor be anxious that you are anxious, nor be disturbed that you are disturbed, but turn naturally to God in sweet and peaceful humility, going so far as to thank him that he has not allowed you to commit still greater faults.

Such sweet and peaceful humility, joined to trust in divine goodness, will calm and pacify you interiorly, and this is your greatest spiritual need at present.

Jean-Pierre de Caussade (1675–1751)[9]

Let all mortal flesh keep silence
  And with fear and trembling stand;
Ponder nothing earthly-minded,
  For with blessing in his hand
Christ our God to earth descendeth,
  Our full homage to demand.

Liturgy of St James, trans. G. Moultrie

If the Lord's being appointed for the fall and resurrection of many is understood in the right way, then the fall will refer to that of the passions and of evil thoughts in each of the faithful, and the resurrection to that of the virtues and of every thought that enjoys God's blessing.

Maximus the Confessor, The Philokalia [10]

10

Humiliation and humility: the way to acceptable behaviour

> Humility is essentially just a true knowledge and appreciation of ourselves, as we really are. It must be obvious that anyone who can really see and experience himself as he is, is bound to be humble.
> (*The Cloud of Unknowing*)

The average person reaches adult life with an emotional knapsack full of memories of the early years of life. These are on the whole likely to be unpleasant because of the emotional reaction they evinced. It seems to be a general rule that the painful episodes of our past life tend to uncover the weak uncertainty of our background, so that we may either hide under a blurred anonymity or else build up an imposing façade of strength whereby we may hope to impress those around us. This subterfuge has its pathetic side, for usually our acquaintances, and even our friends, are fully centred on their own interests, and are only likely to spare a thought for us if our welfare is of obvious consequence to them. In other words, the general public is notoriously self-centred. In practice this obsession with self is virtually inevitable because we are obliged to take care of ourselves and our families immediately; this is our first duty in a civil society.

We are unlikely to contribute much other than disorder to those living close to us if our home is dishevelled and disharmonious. On the other hand, a simple dwelling where love is in evidence radiates peace and concern far beyond its precincts. The value of an intimate relationship in adult life, typically marriage, is primarily the inevitability of learning about one's true nature in a continuous situation where every quirk lies exposed. When an unpleasant character trait is laid bare, our face may redden, our heart may palpitate as if it were failing, and we can barely look our friends in the face. We cannot in fact look at ourselves in the mirror, we are so ashamed. This is the state of *humiliation*. It is a state of self-reproach to such a degree that one is severely incapacitated emotionally, and may go so far as to exclude oneself from all company except for those intimate friends who know one better than one does oneself.

The essence of humiliation is an awareness of acting immorally and then being detected. In other words, humiliation is severely darkened with guilt. One thinks once more of Judas Iscariot, who simply could not bear the consequences of what he had done to Jesus. One may have a little sympathy for Judas, not for what he did but because he has become a convenient scapegoat for the other apostles, who themselves behaved pretty disgustingly when their Master was apprehended. They did not support him in his hour of greatest need, but became heroic after his resurrection and especially after Pentecost. We need not censure them for their faint-heartedness since they were only flesh and blood as we are.

Clearly, Jesus had summed up their characters when he first chose them to be his associates. Early in John's Gospel we read:

> While he was in Jerusalem for Passover many put their trust in him when they saw the signs that he performed. But Jesus for his part would not trust himself to them. He knew them all, and had no need of evidence from others about anyone, for he himself could tell what was in people.[1]

This being so, why did he choose such a motley crew of apostles, none of whom showed heroic qualities at the time of his ministry and one of whom turned traitor? Perhaps because although the twelve apostles were simple countrymen and unlettered in the niceties of theology, they had staunch faith in Jesus and respect for him despite their momentary lapses into fear and cowardice. Jesus not only saw what he might expect from them when their weakness was exposed, acknowledged and forgiven; he also respected their humility, a quality not much in evidence in Judas Iscariot. That was his tragedy. Judas could not face exposure and divine forgiveness, and opted for suicide, an especially unsatisfactory termination of life, in order to escape personal responsibility.

The only one of the apostles who seems to have played a significant part in the proclamation of the Christian faith was Peter.[2] Through

John and Peter, a man lame from birth received a miraculous healing by the Temple gate called Beautiful, where he had sat to beg from people as they went in. He asked for alms but received an amazing healing. Peter extended this miracle to a further promotion of the faith concerning Jesus, at which the chief priests, together with the controller of the Temple and the Sadducees, broke in on them, annoyed because they were proclaiming the resurrection from the dead by teaching the people about Jesus.[3]

The experience of humiliation is potentially useful in character formation. One of the commonest and least attractive features of immature people is their tendency to sit in judgement on others. They occupy a self-created throne of righteousness from which they can lay down the law to those around them. Being merely human, they too are liable to fall from grace; the temptations of worldly life can be irresistible when sexual stimulation, financial reward or social eminence beckon them to dangerous associations. Even a misplaced word can lead to a social disaster, and often something considerably worse is committed. When the fault is exposed the self-righteous person's 'friends' recoil in horror (with a subtle smile of inner disdain and amusement), and leave the unfortunate person to sort out their own business unimpeded. This is rather cruel, but it does have the advantage of throwing the ball into the person's own court. If they have the necessary honesty and courage, they may grow considerably in maturity to become useful members of the community, helping others in concern instead of merely criticizing with withering contempt.

Jesus was obviously humiliated when he was nailed to a cross for three hours in full public view. He was taunted by the onlookers: ' "He saved others: now let him save himself, if this is God's Messiah, his Chosen." The soldiers joined in the mockery and came forward offering him sour wine. "If you are the king of the Jews," they said, "save yourself." '[4]

Jesus suffered grievously, and his suffering became extreme near the end when he cried out, 'My God, my God, why have you forsaken me?'[5] At this point his perfect humanity was overshadowed by his divinity, which carried him through to his death and produced a perfect resurrection appearance on the third day. Jesus' prior humiliation had little effect on his morale on the cross, in this way contrasting with the typical human reaction to shattered confidence. His reaction to personal downfall is common to that of all heroes, because in their hour of destitution they are all close to God even if they claim an atheistic stance.

When one considers some of the outrages committed in God's name, one can appreciate an honest person's dismissal of the very concept of deity. The only way to God is by personal experience, when one is filled with divine grace. A new person arises like a phoenix from the ashes of the old when one knows the joy of God's presence in one's life. This is the way in which a fundamentally sound person arises anew after a crushing blow that has momentarily shattered their self-esteem. The hero is filled with this knowledge from an early age.

Humility is an attitude of regarding oneself with quiet realism. It is an essential component in the character of us all, inasmuch as none of us knows everything, and we are all liable to err from time to time. Conversely, we should respect the opinions of others irrespective of their social background or intellectual capacity. Some opinions, however, are so obviously aberrant that they must be brushed aside promptly for the welfare of the community. One thinks in this respect of the extreme right-wing perversions of recent times, fascism and especially nazism, which are frankly evil. Communism is not in the same category. Its basis is idealistic and potentially good; its failure is consequent on the moral weakness of its leaders. The same is disturbingly true of the history of the great world faiths, including Christianity.

It is interesting that the break-up of European communism, which in itself was a way to political freedom, has not left the general population conspicuously happier. The heavy hand of communist tyranny has been replaced by an oppressive capitalism. Quite a few Eastern Europeans look back with yearning to their communist past when there was a fairly equal distribution of resources and warm bonhomie among the people. No wonder Jesus taught, 'You cannot serve God and Money.'[6] It may be that humankind will never be happy, even were it to have the most radical political programme and enlightened personal care. These would serve only to expose deeper flaws in the body politic. Only a change of heart in each individual, from egotism to altruism, can refashion the face of the world community.

Humility is admirable so long as it does not conflict with self-esteem. If one lacks a good opinion of oneself, one's entire relationship with the world is spoilt. One feels inferior to others, and one's attitude becomes fixed in a warp that can distort one's character almost beyond recognition. One may become obsequious to the 'right' people, toadying to the rich and important, and showing how useful one may be in their service. Admittedly this gross invitation to service or the desire for patronage has a Victorian ring to it, but elements of it still prevail in our social life. It is a time for celebration when one can break free from this encumbrance and be truly oneself. As Shakespeare put it so memorably in *Hamlet*: 'This above all – to thine own self be true, and it must follow, as night the day, thou canst not then be false to any man.'[7]

Humility is seen most positively as an attitude of respect for all humans, irrespective of their background or personal attributes. If this respect can be extended to all living creatures, so much the better. The earth on which we live is worthy of our profound care. Jesus teaches us that God cares for all his creation, from the lilies growing in the fields and the grass which is soon thrown on the stove. We can, then, have complete confidence in God's care for us.[8] We have been given the physical, mental and psychological equipment necessary for our survival in a hazardous world. That we will be bruised, hurt and have periods of doubt and disillusion, is part of our worldly life; if we have the courage and faith to carry on despite all discouragement we shall prevail.

Humility makes no grandiose gestures of strength or defiance, it simply gets on with the work. It may sometimes follow a severe humiliation, when a person's defects of character are fully exposed to view. This may be a necessary sequel to one's inadequate attitude to life, but on occasion it may follow extremely severe, long-continued abuse. If the problem has been one of a wrong personal attitude, one needs to grow in maturity, but if the humiliation has been the result of severe abuse, love is the key to healing. All illusions of strength and personal importance are dispersed and only a weak, trembling human remains. Such an individual has an air of a little child about them; their vulnerability is pathetic to behold. Like a small baby, they seem to have been born naked into a new world – one in which there are no illusions of grandeur or importance.

The atmosphere may be chilling at first but one soon becomes acclimatized. Survival depends on adaptation to a new way of life. It is in fact a relief to lay aside the old persona with its panoply of illusions, and to see instead what one really is as an authentic person. We need not, then, behave immorally to gain advantage. The real joy of life is unselfconscious awareness of the present moment, which is where we meet God directly. And in that presence we may meet something of Christ in ourself: 'Christ in you, the hope of glory.'[9]

Upon Reflection

Humility is just as much the opposite of self-abasement as it is of self-exaltation. To be humble is *not to make comparisons*. Secure in its reality, the self is neither better nor worse, bigger nor smaller, than anything else in the universe. It *is* – is nothing, yet at the same time one with everything. It is in this sense that humility is absolute self-effacement.

To be nothing in the self-effacement of humility, yet, for the sake of the task, to embody *its* whole weight and importance in your bearing, as the one who has been called to undertake it. To give to people, works, poetry, art, what the self can contribute, and to take, simply and freely, what belongs to it by reason of its identity. Praise and blame, the winds of success and adversity, blow over such a life without leaving a trace or upsetting its balance.

Towards this, so help me, God.

Dag Hammarskjöld (1905–61), *Markings*[10]

The world shall never know peace while one man will look at another and pass judgement on him, for this is the seed of war.

But I say to you; when a man can look at another and understand why he is so, and being totally unaffected by what he sees can guide his need, then self will be overcome and peace on earth shall be fulfilled through the heart of Jesus Christ our Lord.

Metropolitan Anthony Bloom, *Living Prayer*[11]

So if in Christ there is anything that will move you, any incentive in love, any fellowship in the Spirit, any warmth or sympathy – I appeal to you, make my joy complete by being of a single mind, one in love, one in heart and one in mind. Nothing is to be done out of jealousy or vanity; instead, out of humility of mind everyone should give preference to others, everyone pursuing not selfish interests but those of others. Make your own the mind of Christ Jesus: Who being in the form of God, did not count equality with God something to be grasped. But he emptied himself, taking the form of a slave, becoming as human beings are; and being in every way like a human being, he was humbler yet, even to accepting death, death on a cross.

Philippians 2.1–8, *New Jerusalem Bible*

He came down to earth from heaven,
　Who is God and Lord of all,
　And his shelter was a stable,
　And his cradle was a stall;
With the poor and mean and lowly,
Lived on earth our Saviour holy ...

And our eyes at last shall see him,
　Through his own redeeming love,
For that Child so dear and gentle
　Is our Lord in heav'n above;
And he leads his children on
To the place where he is gone.
　　　　Mrs C. F. Alexander (1818–95)

11

Fear, failing and forgiveness: the way of spiritual growth

Our courteous Lord does not want his servants to despair because they
fall often and grievously; for our falling does not hinder him in loving
us. (Julian of Norwich, *Revelations of Divine Love*)

When we were very small, our parents seemed to be very friendly, but
when they forbade some action they showed us a different side. If we
persisted in this action their anger was very evident, and we were
afraid of it. This sequence of events must be fairly universal, for the
very young are bound to show their own identity and flout the
restrictions that encompass them. The most painful punishment is the
displeasure of those caring for them; a break in a close relationship is
more wounding than chastisement. The sequence is usually brought
to an end by the spontaneous forgiveness of the parent.

This is right in the case of a very small child, but becomes
inappropriate in older children, who should be made aware that they
are members of the community and dare not flout its rules without
serious repercussions of disapproval. In an adult there might be
complete isolation from their associates, and even their friends, if the
misdemeanour was of sufficient gravity; they would then be 'cut dead'
by the community. It is noteworthy how simple disobedience in a
small child can have increasingly serious implications if it is left
unchecked in older people. It is also noteworthy that the social pain of
just retribution is the heart of its punishment.

Fear is an unpleasant emotion, caused by exposure to danger or the
anticipation of pain, destruction or death, to mention but a few potent
stimuli of this forbidding state of mind. In the situation described
above the fear of punishment is the emotion that steers a person on

the straight and narrow path of decency, and the punishment is primarily social exclusion. A drawback to using fear as a means of enforcing good behaviour is that it is an unstable force. An adventurous type of person will almost automatically devise ways of circumventing the law in order to attain their own ends. The skilled or habitual criminal can be so hardened to fear as to seem to regard imprisonment as a fair price to pay for their antisocial behaviour. Fear is an emotion essential to prevent one endangering one's life through thoughtless actions, and this attitude should be extended to other people with whom one may be associating. However, fear must not be allowed to dominate one's life; it should be tempered with calm awareness so that it is moderated to quiet caution.

The limitation of this apparently sound advice is that it tends to focus the person's attention on their own welfare to the exclusion of the greater world, except in so far as it impinges on their own interests. The cautious person may conceivably escape 'the slings and arrows of outrageous fortune',[1] but they will not experience the heights and depths of love, joy and peace. Their coldness will have the effect of separating them from their fellows. If they marry, this coldness may still persist.

This is not the end of the matter. Life is an ongoing process, and unforeseen events may modify its apparently smooth course when all seems safe and predictable. The operative force, at least on a personal level, is temptation. This is an incitement to wrongdoing which for no clear reason may prove irresistible to a person who usually appears balanced. The clause in the Lord's Prayer, 'Lead us not into temptation but deliver us from evil', is certainly difficult to explain, for it is inconceivable that the creator and lover of the universe should mislead a creature to wrongdoing. It is possible that an erring person may be tempted to invoke divine protection after committing a flagrant offence. This type of religion is sheer hypocrisy, and we should be protected from using the divine name scandalously.

A different translation, which is favoured in some contemporary liturgies, is, 'Do not bring us to the time of trial.' This again is unsatisfactory, because we are tested and strengthened by severe trial, as the saints and martyrs of faith grew inspiringly in stature by experiencing pain or doubt. Did not Jesus himself cry out on the cross, 'Eloi, Eloi, lama sabachtani?' which means, 'My God, my God, why have you forsaken me?'

Hearing this, some of the bystanders said, 'Listen! He is calling Elijah.' Someone ran and soaked a sponge in sour wine and held it to his lips on the end of a stick. 'Let us see', he said, 'if Elijah will come and take him down.' Then Jesus gave a loud cry and died; and the curtain of the temple was torn in two from top to bottom. When the centurion who was standing opposite him saw how he died, he said, ' 'Truly' this man must have been a son of God.'[2]

Jesus most certainly did not escape the time of trial, and nor did the host of martyrs who died in the genocidal atrocities of our own time, many of whom were not Christians. It is one thing to identify oneself boldly with a great religious leader and formulate stirring dogmas about his or her antecedents, but quite another to follow the way of the illuminated person, if necessary to martyrdom.

Failure need not always be due to a character defect; it may follow the natural course of an external process, for instance the recurrence of an illness after a long period of remission when the patient and medical attendant alike believed that cure had been obtained. The classical example is cancer, which may appear as a secondary deposit, or metastasis, years after the primary tumour has been completely eradicated. Evidently some cancer cells were carried by the bloodstream or the lymphatics further afield before the primary focus was removed, and remained dormant until local conditions favoured proliferation.

If we consider the history of humankind, there have been peaks of civilization which could indeed have presaged a real world millennium, a period of good government, great happiness and permanent prosperity. Examples of this are the period of Jewish return from Babylonian exile; the first three centuries after Jesus' death before Christianity became an imperial religion and power took precedence over spirituality; the later Middle Ages and the Renaissance; and the Enlightenment of the eighteenth century which extended to the early twentieth century. The process of civilization failed disastrously with the advent of the First World War and the subsequent horrors of fascism, nazism, the Second World War and a subsequent fifty-five years of regional warfare and genocide. Through this appalling darkness there have been sparks of great hope, as mentioned in chapter 10, but only a trust in an overseeing providence whom we call God gives us much confidence in the future.

When we have been hurt by a careless blow we are, understandably, very angry. If the action was clearly accidental, the offending party should apologize at once and act to redress the injury. If this is true of a physical injury, it is equally valid for a slip of the tongue. It is difficult for some people to feel deeply sorry for what they have done. There is also a type of apologizing which is so glib that it simply demonstrates the person's general irresponsibility and lack of consideration.

How should we react in such a situation? The Christian answer is forgiveness: the first word of Jesus on the cross is traditionally, 'Father, forgive them; they do not know what they are doing.'[3] When Peter came to Jesus and asked him how often he was to forgive his brother if he went on wronging him – as many as seven times? Jesus replied, 'I do not say seven times but seventy times seven.'[4] St Paul reminds us of the universality of wrongdoing: 'for all alike have sinned, and are deprived of the divine glory.'[5] In practice this admirable advice to extend unlimited forgiveness has meaning only if it comes from the heart. As noted above, forgiving, like apologizing, can be merely a form of words said by rote without any deeper conviction. How then should we forgive?

There should first of all be an attitude of forgiveness in one's heart; one should not be forced or cajoled into forgiveness by a well-meaning third party. In fact, many self-appointed peacemakers have an urge to interfere with and manipulate other people. The person who has been hurt should wait for an apology from the guilty party, and when an overture is forthcoming it is wise as well as generous to receive it. People who bear perpetual grudges become warped and unpleasant in their relationships generally. Their *bête noire* occupies their thoughts far too pervasively, and may become such a persistent topic of conversation that even their friends begin to flinch from their company. They become fearful bores.

Once the guilty party is at peace with the person they have injured, it is wise to close a past wound with an act of celebration. There should be no lingering distrust or antipathy. These negative emotions may be cancelled by the apology rendered at the time of reconciliation. If there was a warm relationship before the break, it may resume with the same intensity soon afterwards. Should one forgive a person who does not apologize or seek reconciliation? Jesus taught that we should forgive to an unlimited degree, but we cannot force another person to receive forgiveness. If, for instance, they believe they were in the right or, worse still, if they are filled with utter contempt for the injured party, no forgiveness will impinge upon them.

The way forward is to allow a place for reconciliation in one's heart, even if it cannot be expressed to the person concerned. The parable of the Prodigal Son is helpful in this respect.[6] The father's love does not weaken when the younger son leaves home and wastes his inheritance in dissolute living. The young man returns home in deep shame, but his father is lost in rejoicing that an apparently dead son has returned to life. He is received royally. This is how we should remember and treat those who are incapable of receiving forgiveness: keep them in our prayers until they undergo a change of heart, just as the father in the parable never lost spiritual contact with his irresponsible son.

One cannot forgive until love flourishes in one's own heart. The secret of living abundantly is to be able to give of oneself to others in need at all times. The Gospels give an impressive account of the life and ministry of Jesus. He did not spare himself, yet there is no feeling of cynicism or irritation:

> Come to me, all who are weary and whose load is heavy; I will give you rest. Take my yoke upon you, and learn from me, for I am gentle and humble-hearted; and you will find rest for your souls. For my yoke is easy to wear, my load is light.[7]

Jesus lightens the heavy yoke of the Law which is magnified by the observances of the Pharisees. His humble-heartedness is a consequence of holy poverty for the sake of others. His greatness is shown in his capacity to empathize with all manner of humankind.

Upon Reflection

Forgiveness breaks the chain of causality because he who 'forgives' you – out of love – takes upon himself the consequences of what *you* have done. Forgiveness, therefore, always entails a sacrifice.

The price you must pay for your own liberation through another's sacrifice, is that you in turn must be willing to liberate in the same way, irrespective of the consequences to yourself.

Dag Hammarskjöld, *Markings*[8]

Dear Lord and Father of mankind,
    Forgive our foolish ways!
Reclothe us in our rightful mind,
In purer lives thy service find,
    In deeper reverence praise.

Drop thy still dews of quietness,
  Till all our strivings cease;
Take from our souls the strain and stress,
And let our ordered lives confess
  The beauty of Thy peace.

J. G. Whittier (1807–92)[9]

Everything good in you originates from God, everything evil, spoilt
and corrupt originates in yourself. Set aside then, nothingness and sin,
evil habits and inclinations, abysmal weakness and wretchedness. These
are your portion. These originate in, and unquestionably belong to,
you.

Everything else – the body and its energies, the soul and its senses,
the modicum of good you have performed – is God's portion. It so
manifestly belongs to him that you realize you cannot claim one whit of
it as yours, nor feel one grain of complacency, without being guilty of
theft and larceny against God.

At frequent intervals repeat interiorly: 'Lord, have pity upon me;
with you all things are possible.' There is nothing better or more simple
than this; nothing more is needed to call forth his powerful help. Hold
powerfully to these practices and inclinations. God will do the rest
without your perceiving it.

Jean-Pierre de Caussade [10]

O Lord Jesus Christ, Son of the living God,
have mercy upon me, a sinner.

The Jesus Prayer

12

Ages and stages of the spiritual path: the education of the will

The doctrine of pure love can only be learnt by God's action, not by any effort of our own spirit. God instructs the heart not by means of ideas, but by pains and contradictions. (Jean-Pierre de Caussade)

W. R. Inge, the redoubtable dean of St Paul's cathedral in the earlier part of the twentieth century, divided the phases of spiritual exploration in an enquiring adult into three distinct partitions: action, reflection and love. The first embraces positive, vigorous activity; the second, extending from the age of about forty to approximately sixty-five, involves a quieter, more sedate approach, still very strong and positive in one's opinions but rather less emphatic; and then a third, final phase of quiet tranquillity, when one can retire gracefully into oneself and view secular matters with a mature, serene, conscious awareness.

This serenity is the quintessence of love. It has little 'side' to it, and feels no need to justify itself. Of course it has not resigned its concern, let alone its responsibility, into the hands of others, but there is a trust and reliance which makes the third phase one of peace and love. One begins to feel that one can trust other people with increasing love and discernment.

Trust and love develop increasingly warmly. The secret of their growing warmth is a tacit awareness that the approach of the end of life brings a close understanding of the meaning and understanding of existence; that, as John Keats put it, life is a 'vale of soul-making'. We are here to fertilize our little patch of beauty, of fecundity, so that it may expand into a small plot of loveliness to enrich a younger generation when we have entered into our 'eternal reward'. To effect this great achievement of plotting out a vale of soul-making, we need to have a plan of action at our disposal, and this is where the will to serve is of such importance.

Going back to the first of Inge's three prerequisites – action, reflection and love – the will is very important in deliberate action. It becomes crucially important for a life of selfish concern, for then our lives are centred on what we personally consider our own welfare, to the exclusion of all other considerations. It is often miscalled 'will-power'. But as age and experience assuage our self-centred demands, so we are able to relinquish our own desire for gratification and lessen the craving of a powerful appetite for immediate satisfaction. Let it be said at once that no impropriety is to be attached to a vigorous carnal appetite provided it is under firm moral control.

An Analysis of the Will

The will is frequently envisaged as the forceful action of the dominating mind that is determined to have its own way, to do what it has set out to achieve, and to exercise its own selfish power over outer events, whether these are the shape of individual personality or the more pliable occurrences that affect the course of human life. In fact, the will is considerably more pervasive than this. It thrusts itself forward when all is going well, when the things of the world are progressing encouragingly. It 'gets things going' and 'keeps them moving'. It does not waste time.

A deficient aspect of the will is its inability to restrain its action. Once it is mobilized there is no limit to its activity, and the results can be disastrous. Therefore the ages and stages of the spiritual path have the vital function of educating the will, which on its own might run amok and lead to incalculable damage.

Youth is the period of life that has no qualms about its own rightness. By and large it veers in a decidedly dogmatic, impetuous direction. It has to learn better manners when it is forced to admit that it is not the arbiter of all judgements. The young tend to know everything and are often severely judgemental. This is not meant to be a severe, let alone harsh, assessment of the earlier years of life; it is simply a recognition of ignorance based on a lack of deeper experience. With the advent of age greater wisdom accrues.

The ages of reflection, and especially love, bring with them mellowness and a deepening assessment of life. One begins to see matters, both personal and communal, with a greater sympathy. One can regard world issues on a broader canvas, and no longer remain dogmatic and intolerant. This is the foundation of civilized behaviour, of caring and of love. It is at this stage that concerted mutual action can become possible. Now at last people can live and work together as responsible units in a caring, sacrificing community.

It should be borne in mind that the will is the action of the soul. It is distinct from 'will-power'. It is the way of love that leads one along the path. It brings one to the divine presence, and in its embrace it guides one straight to God. This is the way forward to the path of enlightenment. It is on this path that the ages and stages of the spiritual path and the education of the will come together harmoniously. The will does not control the paths imperiously, rather it eases the way gently and firmly. Only when the ages and stages of a person's spiritual maturity are fully aligned with the development of their will can the individual attain true maturity. The two later stages tend in fact to run in parallel. As one grows in spiritual depth, so the will more and more directs one's development. The three ages and stages of life each have their own joy. We are wise if we allow each to have their breathing space in which to grow and expand in their magnitude.

Upon Reflection

'Violent emotional fervours', says Hilton, 'do not belong to a high state, but are rather characteristic of beginners, who for the littleness and weakness of their souls cannot bear the smallest touch of God.' This is quite in accordance with what other authorities tell us; though they more often suggest that these rapturous joys are given by God as an encouragement to those who are just beginning to advance on the way of holiness.

W. R. Inge (1860–1954), *Studies of English Mystics* [1]

Humility and distress free man from every sin, the former by cutting out the passions of the soul, the latter those of the body . . .

As much as it is easier to sin in thought than in deed, so is a war with thoughts more exacting than one with things.

Maximus the Confessor, 'Chapters on Love' [2]

Jesus Who is both love and light is in this darkness . . . He is in the soul as its labouring for light in desire and longing, but He is not yet in it as its resting in love.

Walter Hilton, *The Ladder of Perfection* [3]

The will of man has the nature of divine freedom; has the nature of eternity, and the nature of omnipotence in it; because it is what it is, and has what it has, as a spark, a ray, a genuine birth of the eternal, free, omnipotent will of God. And therefore, as the will of God is superior to, and rules over all nature; so the will of man, derived from the will of God, is superior to, and rules over all his own nature. And thence it is, that as to itself, and so far as its own nature reaches, it has the freedom and omnipotence of that will from which it is descended; and can have or receive nothing, but what itself does, and works, in and to itself.

William Law, *The Way to Divine Knowledge* [4]

13

The prosaic encounter with God: the discipline of dailyness

Our everyday life is the gift by means of which we are meant to draw ever nearer to holiness. (Donald Nicholl)

The encounter with God as a conscious reality is the basis of a mystical experience. The essence of such an experience is unity; the diverse and often conflicting elements of earthly life are embraced in a vibrant love in which all are raised from discord to a single focus of light which radiates love and peace. No one who knows this encounter returns to what they were before, for now their whole being is centred on the presence of God. Egotism declines and a broad, glowing altruism fills its place.

An essential feature of a genuine encounter with God is an easing of earlier attitudes of rugged, somewhat intransigent individualism, and a fostering of increasingly strong bonds of affinity towards a number of people with distinctly diverse characters. In other words, our relationship with God is reflected in our relationships with our fellows. This in turn is shown in a softening of our attitude to the entire world of nature. If we know God, our soul (or heart, in the language of metonymy) expands and vibrates in sympathy with our neighbour, who, in accord with the parable of the Good Samaritan,[1] is everybody we meet in the course of the day. In the routine of heedless mundane activity we tend to be so centred on our concerns that we remain oblivious of the needs of even those near to us unless these people directly affect our lives. When our souls are touched by suffering or compassion towards the passing stranger, we awaken from our customary apathy and move sympathetically towards them, at first to individuals but later on to an increasing number of those in need.

We could go even further and assert that a person who has a spontaneous feeling of love for their fellows and concern for animal welfare knows God in their soul even if they deny with their mind any belief in the divine. Conversely, a person who parades their religion while behaving in an uncaring way towards those whom they meet from day to day, and showing scant regard for the world of nature, illustrates the total inadequacy of a religious commitment without any corresponding concern for their neighbours, both human and animal. 'Not everyone who says to me "Lord, Lord" will enter the kingdom of Heaven, but only those who do the will of my heavenly Father.'[2]

To know the nature of God's will was a problem for some Christians from the beginning, and especially when the faith attained imperial supremacy in Rome some three hundred years later. 'When Constantine saw a vision of the cross declaring "In this sign conquer" he read it literally. He saw the Christian faith was more powerful for imperial purposes precisely in the sense he understood power,' writes David Martin.[3] Proselytism always seemed to be the most urgent duty. Conversion to faith in the martyr Jesus of Nazareth was preached by Peter in his inaugural pronouncement at Pentecost, when the gift of tongues (*glossolalia*) had animated the apostles, the first Jews who had known the wonder of Jesus. The whole episode is described in Acts 2. It is summed up thus: 'Repent, and be baptized, every one of you . . . then your sins will be forgiven and you will receive the gift of the Holy Spirit', and, 'Save yourselves from this crooked age.'[4]

The immediate result was seen in an impressive increase in the number of converts: 'All the believers agreed to hold everything in common: they began to sell their property and possessions and distribute to everyone according to his need.'[5] This account bears a resemblance to the saying of Karl Marx: 'From each according to his abilities, to each according to his needs.'[6] But Marx also said, 'Religion is the opium of the people.'[7] It is obvious that Marx's ideas about social rectitude were intellectual, and it is equally inevitable that Marxist communism may start with high ideals, but will in due course proceed to a personal struggle for political power. This has been demonstrated amply in Europe in the twentieth century, with the result that communism was rejected outright before the century ended. China along with Cuba and North Korea at present have communist governments, but at the end of the day these too will fail. No human system survives that does not acknowledge the centrality of the divine. So the final two verses of Acts 2 record the believers' joyful piety both at the Temple and in their homes.[8] It is not surprising that 'day by day the Lord added new converts to their number'.

The need to be saved is especially emphasized in evangelical Christianity. Salvation is described theologically as deliverance from sin and all its consequences, with a subsequent admission to heaven, brought about by Christ. One's conversion may be as beautiful as that of the first disciples, but what happens afterwards? If conversion is genuine and not merely induced by coercion or group emotion, there is an apparent change in the convert's attitude and general behaviour. Inwardly there is a peace that does indeed pass understanding, which allows creativity to proceed with a quiet glow of joy. There is less personal desire and more caring for others, not only those belonging to one's own circle but also for many whom one previously would have completely ignored. One's desire becomes centred on the preservation of the world and the healing of social dissension. We learn that the more freely we can give of ourselves to those in need, the richer we become in those things which outlast the body, such as integrity, wisdom and love. Indeed, we begin to know eternity when we have put the ego to rest once it has engaged in the immediate activities of the present hour. Prayer is known as the most holy activity, inasmuch as the thinking mind is stilled and the soul is enabled to communicate directly with God.

This apparent quietness is our part in the divine conversation, when we can learn immortal truth by giving our attention to God's summons to life and then applying the message in our subsequent resolve. The stilling of the personality is an essential requirement for its growth to maturity, for then it no longer needs to assert itself, proving it has the right answers to every problem, impressing the world with its power, and holding forth at length on every subject. A quiet type of person may, of course, be merely concealing their shyness, embarrassment or sheer ignorance. It is not difficult for an astute observer to recognize the emotional basis of their silence. But there is also a quiet type of confidence that rests on a deeper certainty, that all *is* well even now, not merely *will be* as was revealed to Julian of Norwich. This is a modest encounter with God 'to whom all hearts are open, all desires known, and from whom no secrets are hidden', to quote from the *Book of Common Prayer* and the *Alternative Service Book 1980*, in the order for Holy Communion in the Anglican rite.[9]

As we grow in spiritual sensitivity, so we are blessed with this quiet awareness of God. It is the mysticism of the common life. Its fruits are those of the Holy Spirit listed in chapter 3, especially love, joy and peace. There is ceaseless activity in one's own work for the benefit of everybody; personal ambition is subsumed under the category of service to other people in one's vicinity, which may ultimately extend to the entire community. The great mystics are ever-living examples of this way of life, and among them there is none greater than the Christ and the Buddha.

A famous mystic of the common life was Brother Lawrence, a Carmelite lay brother who entered a Discalced Carmelite monastery in 1649, where he was given charge of the kitchen and led a life of almost constant recollection. This is an attitude of attentiveness to God and to oneself. The idea that the soul becomes dissipated through its concern for worldly things and should 'collect itself' into itself to concentrate on its spiritual purpose occurs in Plato,[10] and it recurs in various forms in the church Fathers and in medieval writers. St Teresa of Avila treats recollection as a kind, or stage, of prayer. Selections of Brother Lawrence's conversations and letters under the title *The Practice of the Presence of God* have had a wide reception as a spiritual classic.

He writes: 'The time of business does not differ from the time of prayer; and in the noise and clutter of my kitchen, while several people are at the same time calling for different things, I possess God in as great tranquillity as if I were upon my knees at the Blessed Sacrament.'[11] The explanation of this constant awareness of God is contained in the advice, 'We should establish ourselves in a sense of God's Presence, by continually conversing with him.'[12]

The prerequisite for this divine encounter is a total submission of the self to the Other. On a more restricted plane we can effect a close communion with our fellows also; we seek less to impose on them and more to support them for our mutual benediction. Unfortunately a considerable number of people are unable to attain this standard of concern for their fellow mortals. They cannot be driven along the path of sanctity, and have necessarily to pursue their chosen way of self-interest. But the end is a cul-de-sac. 'What does anyone gain by winning the whole world at the cost of destroying himself?'[13] Bitter experience may serve to open their eyes to a greater reality, and then they may yield to the omnipotence of God and his divine grace. Once self-interest has been relaxed, the loving concern of God is allowed into the soul of the previously self-sufficient individual, and a new person is born.

The conversion of Saul of Tarsus is a striking case in point.[14] He was subsequently to be called Paul and was filled with the Holy Spirit.[15] This is the prosaic encounter with God; it may be part of a natural mystical temperament as in the case of Brother Lawrence, or follow a tempestuous experience as in the conversion of St Paul or the younger son in the story commonly called the Prodigal Son.[16] It is prosaic in that the divine communion may start on a high peak of wonder, but then emerges undramatically into the routine events of common, everyday life. Our responses to the events of today are the test of our spirituality.

Upon Reflection

To avoid dissipation in the tasks that your obedience sets you to do, you need but to go about them placidly, showing neither anxiety nor over-eagerness; while to perform them in this way you have, says St Francis de Sales, but to do them wholly out of love for God and obedience to God.

For, the same saint adds, since this love is gentle and persuasive, all that it inspires us to do has the same nature. But when self-love intervenes with its desire for success and self-satisfaction – that desire is its constant companion – first it imports an element of human activity and eagerness, and then anxiety and grief.

Be that as it may, you will tell me, I am quite convinced that these tasks hinder advancement. When, dear Sister, we love only the love of God, we wish to advance only as much as God wishes; we abandon ourselves to his divine Providence for our spiritual progress.

Jean-Pierre de Caussade, Fire of Divine Love [17]

He was very sensible of his faults, but not discouraged by them. He confessed them to God, but did not plead against him to excuse them. When he had done so, he peaceably resumed his usual practice of love and adoration.

Brother Lawrence, Daily Readings from Brother Lawrence [18]

I must desire my advancement and perfection only so far as God wishes it and by the means that he wishes. Such a desire can only be calm and peaceful, even when it is full of vehemence and fervour.

But there is another desire for our perfection that springs from pride and an immoderate love of our own excellence. This does not depend upon God: consequently it is restless and forever agitated.

Our need to surrender our soul to the first of these and our need to put all our energy into defeating the second are equally great. All desire for our advancement, therefore, however holy it appears, must be curbed the moment eagerness, restlessness or perturbation enters into it. Such results can only come from the devil, since all that comes from God leaves us tranquil interiorly.

Jean-Pierre de Caussade *ibid.* [19]

The prayer life built in response to the feelings of the moment is as a house built on sand; it is powerless against the wind and the storm. That which is built on the fortress of the will – not despising the emotions, for their right functioning is essential to a full Christian life, yet seeing them as subordinate to the will – that is the house which can withstand times of testing when they come.

Robert Llewelyn, *Our Duty and our Joy* [20]

Breathe on me, Breath of God,
    Fill me with life anew,
That I may love what thou dost love,
    And do what thou wouldst do.

Breathe on me, Breath of God,
    Until my heart is pure;
Until with thee I will one will,
    To do and to endure.

Breathe on me, Breath of God,
    Till I am wholly thine;
Until this earthly part of me
    Glows with thy fire divine.

Breathe on me, Breath of God:
    So shall I never die,
But live with thee the perfect life
    Of thine eternity.

E. Hatch (1835–89)

14

The Word of God: creation and regeneration

Just as all die in Adam, so in Christ all will be brought to life.
(1 Corinthians 15.22, *New Jerusalem Bible*)

The writer of the fourth Gospel begins his account of the Incarnation thus:

> In the beginning was the Word, and the Word was with God, and the
> Word was God. The same was in the beginning with God. All things
> were made by him; and without him was not anything made that was
> made. In him was life; and the life was the light of men. And the light
> shineth in darkness; and the darkness comprehendeth it not.[1]

The light has never been extinguished by the darkness, and has
eternally enlightened humanity. But few respond to the full radiance
of the light; its illumination does not penetrate beneath the surface of
the personality, where its energy is expended on selfish attainment.
To those who are permeable to the light there is an awakening of the
soul, where God is known. Then that person in turn becomes a bearer
of the light, bringing the light of God to others.

Jesus' soul was so clear of all self-concern that he was a perfect
image of the divine nature. Therefore it is right to call him the Son of
God.

> That was the true Light, which lighteth every man that cometh into the
> world. He was in the world, and the world was made by him, and the
> world knew him not. He came unto his own, and his own received
> him not. But as many as received him, to them gave he power to
> become the sons of God, even to them that believe on his name:
> Which were born, not of blood, nor of the will of the flesh, nor of the

will of man, but of God. And the Word was made flesh, and dwelt among us, (and we beheld his glory, the glory as of the only begotten of the Father,) full of grace and truth.[2]

The Word (or *Logos*) is described in the Old Testament not only as a medium of communication, but also as a source of creative power, as in the first chapter of Genesis and the Psalms: 'The word of the Lord created the heavens; all the host of heaven was formed at his command.'[3] In the writings of the prophets the Word of the Lord is presented as having an almost independent existence.[4] In Hellenistic Judaism the concept of the *Logos* as an independent hypostasis (individual reality) was further developed, and the *Logos* also came to be associated with the figure of Wisdom.[5]

In the New Testament the term in its technical sense is confined to the Johannine writings.[6] As already quoted in the Prologue of the fourth Gospel, the *Logos* is described as God from eternity, the Creative Word, who became incarnate in the man Jesus (the Christ) of Nazareth.

From this cradle of Christian orthodoxy there should arise a contemporary doctrine of humanity. It may be pleasing to immerse oneself in historical statements of the faith, especially when couched in the language of the Authorized Version of the Bible, and then to lapse through a phase of *laissez-faire* (the practice of governmental abstention from interference in the workings of the market) to one of *laissez-aller* (unconstrained freedom, with an absence of any restriction of liberty). The end is the destruction of a civilized society. The great religions of the world have come through individuals divinely inspired to lead their fellows once more through the path of discipline to a way beyond the isolated self to the communal self, where personality plays second fiddle to the community. The end of this movement is a knowledge of God, where creativity blossoms like a spring flower, and the fruits of the Spirit bless the entire society. Unfortunately, after a natal period of religious orthodoxy a clerical establishment is likely to take over authority. Being essentially human, the figures composing the ruling party tend to live by the word rather than the spirit of the doctrine, until such time as the inspiration of the founder is largely overlaid by the additional word of those who govern. These may impose a rule of rigid self-control in obedience to their own will, all in the name of God and the founder of the religion. The result is a fundamentalism in which the written word takes over as interpreted literally by an intolerant group who make use of it according to their immediate need. The end of this perversion may be persecution of dissidents and civil war, even wars between nations. It is no surprise that in many Western countries churchgoing has declined of late. Whether this trend is lamentable or not depends on the disposition of the individual. If there is an awareness of God deep within one, it may be advisable not to attend public worship until one finds a church in which one feels at home. A church with a strongly fundamentalist theology may not be suitable.

The fact that churchgoing has declined recently is due in part to a growing dissatisfaction with the narrowness of presentation of the faith. The fundamental questions of life mentioned in chapter 4 are not often confronted directly until one's own circumstances force one to ponder more deeply, and then one may feel very alone even if one is accompanied by a host of friends. It is in this consideration that the importance of public worship is evident. In such an environment we are in the company of like-minded people among whom we can make our own special contribution, the heart of which is love in our own setting. Private worship, while essential in its own, right, is not complete until it is shared with at least one other person: 'For where two or three meet together in my name, I am there among them.'[7] It may be that when public worship attains sufficient depth, discerning worshippers will return to regular churchgoing.

At the present time a 'word' has come from the New Age. This ideology is replete with 'aliens' from outer space, spectacular psychic phenomena, an assurance of reincarnation, and communication with many extraterrestrial entities including God himself. While it would be unwise as well as uncharitable to belittle all these beliefs wholesale, it must be admitted that they await objective confirmation. As St Paul reminds us, 'Satan himself masquerades as an angel of light.' He continues, 'so it is easy enough for his agents to masquerade as agents of good'.[8] When one has been exposed to New Age certainties, one thanks God for the 'great cloud of witnesses' that we have considered in chapter 5.

Is the Word limited to Jesus Christ? What about other great souls like the saints of Islam, Hinduism and Buddhism? Some Christians will shake their heads firmly and negatively at once. The contemporary spirituality of the Western world will affirm the divinity of all these saints. It would not be absolutely perverse to affirm the divinity of any person irrespective of their character and occupation.

We remember once more George Fox's comment that there is 'that of God in every man'[9] and St Paul's proclamation that, 'to them [God's people] he chose to make known what a wealth of glory is offered to the Gentiles in this secret purpose: Christ, in you, the hope of glory.'[10]

This does not mean that all the higher religions are of equal value. The validity of a religion has in the end to be assessed by the lives of those who observed its tenets while on earth. 'A good tree cannot bear bad fruit, or a poor tree sound fruit. A tree that does not yield sound fruit is cut down and thrown on the fire. That is why I say you will recognize them by their fruit.'[11] The fruits of the Spirit [12] are the criteria by which a person's life is evaluated.

We are created by the Word of God, and regenerated by living dangerously in the present moment, being alert to those around us (the whole world no less) and helping those in need. The final word is acceptance as we prepare to leave our mortal body and travel closer to God, when our spiritual vision clears to see what is unimaginable.

Dietrich Bonhoeffer learnt much about this as he lay in prison awaiting his execution:

> To be a Christian does not mean to be religious in a particular way, to cultivate some particular form of asceticism (as a sinner, a penitent, or a saint), but to be a man. It is not some religious act that makes a Christian what he is, but participation in the suffering of God in the life of the world. It is only by living completely in this world that one learns to believe. One must abandon every attempt to make something of oneself, whether it be a saint, a converted sinner, a churchman, a righteous man or an unrighteous one, a sick man or a healthy one. This is what I mean by worldliness – taking life in one's stride, with all its duties and problems, its successes and failures, its experiences and helplessness.[13]

Upon Reflection

We might quote Thomas Merton: 'St Thérèse's little way is an explicit rejection of any exalted or sublime notion tending to cut man off from his ordinary existence or to divide him into halves, one half entrusted to the angels, the other roaming in this vale of tears' (Introduction to *The Way of Chuang Tzu*).

Bernard Bro O.P., *The Little Way*[14]

Her mission is to offer herself to Love so that it might take possession of her and transform her. At last she has found rest, even if Love will keep her on the move until the day of her death and after that, since she will continue her mission in heaven.

Jean Lafrance, *My Vocation is Love: Thérèse of Lisieux* [15]

Love alone can make us pleasing to God, so I desire no other treasure. Jesus has chosen to show me the only way which leads to the Divine Furnace of love; it is the way of child-like self-surrender, the way of a child who sleeps, afraid of nothing, in its father's arms. 'Whosoever is a little one, let him come unto Me' (Proverbs 9.4), says the Holy Spirit through the lips of Solomon, and the same Spirit of Love tells us also that 'to him that is little, mercy is granted' (Wisdom 6.7).

John Nelson (ed.), *The Arms of Love, with St Thérèse of Lisieux* [16]

In order that the dispositions of the Gospel and the things of the Holy Spirit may develop in us, their author has to be born in us.

Gregory of Nyssa, *Against Eunomius* [17]

Fear not the coming of your God; fear not his friendship. He will not straiten you when he comes; rather he will enlarge you. So that you might know that he will enlarge you he not only promised to come, saying, 'I will dwell with them,' but he also promised to enlarge you, adding, 'and I will walk with them'. You see then, if you love, how much room he gives you. Fear is a suffering that oppresses us. But look at the immensity of love. 'God's love has been poured into our hearts' (Romans 5.5).'

Augustine of Hippo (354–430), *Sermons* [18]

One day I saw three monks insulted and humiliated in the same way at the same moment. The first felt he had been cruelly hurt; he was distressed but managed not to say anything. The second was happy for himself but grieved for the one who had insulted him. The third thought only of the harm suffered by his neighbour, and wept with the most ardent compassion. The first was prompted by fear; the second was urged on by the hope of reward; the third was moved by love.

John Climacus (c. 570–649), *The Ladder of Divine Perfection* [19]

15

The sequel to a life: the four last things

Neither death nor life ... nor anything in all creation can separate us from the love of God in Christ Jesus our Lord. (Romans 8.38–9)

In traditional Christianity the four last things are death, judgement, heaven and hell.

The end of all mortal life is death; this was alluded to in chapter 4 in connection with the fate of the body when the person dies. It would seem that our time on earth, a mere trice even if to live to be a hundred were a usual event, is here to aid in the development of our character for the tests ahead of it. These we do not know with accuracy, while our temporal, rational experience is limited to the physical environment in which we are anchored while the body is alive.

That there are other modes of communication is known to everyone through the experience of dreaming. More debatable is experience of extrasensory communication from other living sources, and also from those who appear to communicate from a discarnate background beyond this mortal life, which may, according to the belief of the recipient, come from a source in the world of the great majority who are now deceased.

In the end we have to make up our minds individually. Extra-sensory communication, even if factually valid, might be merely an error from a fallible source in the intermediate realm, and so beyond the simple verification we take for granted in mundane intercourse. With these sensible provisos, and armed with the divine revelation common to the world's collective mystical information, it is possible to construct an extremely plausible account of the soul's experience after its detachment from its body. According to the spiritual development of the individual, their discarnate soul might be amazed to experience life in a new milieu. Dogmatic atheism will yield to reveal a presence in the midst of which the soul will view itself and its previous incarnate life with unremitting accuracy.

This is the basis of the 'Last Judgement' that is traditionally the second of the 'four last things'. For the righteous soul it will be an experience of relief and consolation, so that no matter how painful the stress of the previous life may have been, there is now the peace of welcome rest. The three parables of the kingdom of Heaven which constitute Matthew 25 illustrate the Judgement graphically: those who have been prepared through the long watches of the night, who have employed their gifts profitably, and who have cared for their fellows when they were destitute and alone, are welcomed with joy to the heavenly kingdom. On the other hand, those who were not prepared when the bridegroom arrived later than expected, who had not used their gifts profitably, and who showed no concern for their fellows in a state of distress, are summarily excluded from fellowship (or communion) with other people.

A characteristic mode of expression in Matthew's vocabulary is, 'Throw him out into the dark, where there will be wailing and grinding of teeth.'[1] In a somewhat similar vein the door is shut against the dilatory girls in the parable of the wedding banquet,[2] and those who have remained unmoved by the suffering of their fellow creatures are sentenced to eternal punishment.[3] These three dire accounts of irreversible punishment are the basis of the traditional concept of hell.

It is clear that heaven and hell have no spatial reality, because the soul is not related to a dead body (which undergoes progressive decay within a matter of days in the usual course of events). Heaven and hell are states of mind which we can, and indeed do, experience in the present life. The basic concept of heaven is a relief from suffering, an absence of isolation, and mutual acceptance. There is complete trust, so that we no longer have to guard against violation, whether of our belongings or of our personality. This relief is a glorious experience of openness, and the presence of God is instantaneous.

It proves its origin by its life-transforming quality. Hence the Lord's Prayer commences (in the familiar words of the Authorized Version of the Bible): 'Our Father which art in heaven, Hallowed be thy name. Thy kingdom come. Thy will be done in earth, as it is in heaven.'[4] The experience of heaven is one of pure grace, but it will come to the person open to receive it. As the blessed person knows, the experience is not designed for personal gratification but for communal sharing. The way is that of service in this life and no doubt also in the life ahead after the body has completed its earthly task.

The experience of hell is traditionally regarded as God's punishment on those whose lives were evil. But some mystics, prominent among whom have been Julian of Norwich and William Law, have stressed the pure love of God. The wrath that is such a prominent feature of our world is of human origin, for there is only love in the divine nature. It seems obvious even to lesser individuals like ourselves that a God of love would not condemn the majority of his human creation to eternal damnation. Such an action would not merely be grossly unloving; it would be an admission of failure on God's part, in the magnificent process of creation, that a large proportion of his human creatures should be totally incapable of salvation. That all have sinned, and are 'justified by God's free grace alone, through his act of liberation in the person of Jesus Christ',[5] was mentioned in chapter 4. But will all sinners accept this glorious amnesty?

The more liberal believer tends to play down the terrors of hell. Quoting Julian of Norwich's celebrated illumination from chapter 27 of her *Revelations of Divine Love*, 'Sin is necessary, but all shall be well, and all shall be well, and all manner of thing shall be well', the temptation is all too easy to fold one's hands in an attitude of comfortable complacency. In fact, Julian was not spared her share of sufferings, but was able at the end of her Revelations to see that Love was their meaning. There is no obvious explanation of human evil, which was illustrated in the twentieth century by the actions against humanity of Adolf Hitler, as wicked a person as any who has set foot on the earth.

Ultimately, evil cannot be simply eradicated. The monster can easily be killed, but it is only the body that perishes. The inner form, the soul, is immortal, and it is to this that our attention needs to be directed. The most perverted soul could conceivably continue its subversive activity in an afterlife state. Those who work as exorcists learn to make contact with such lost souls, and by direct communication bring them to a full understanding of their predicament. The key is always love; only those who can give love freely are capable of prayer which is efficacious in delivering lost souls out of hell into the light of rational sight.

Hell is not a place of punishment created by an angry God. It is simply an atmosphere of total exclusion from any living company. It is as if one has ceased to exist, and this terrifying state will persist indefinitely until the erring soul has come to a full acknowledgement of its sinfulness and shows genuine repentance. An exorcist may effect the saving contact that sets the soul on the proper course. This deliverance (a better term than exorcism) is a specialized ministry, which is dangerous except in the hands of dedicated servants of God. The important point is that the agent that precipitates hell is not God, whose nature is always to have mercy, but the individual himself or herself. The selfish (sinful) way of life of such individuals serves to isolate them progressively from their fellows, and when they die their possessions, like their body, fall away from them also.

The law never alters.

> Make no mistake about this: God is not to be fooled; everyone reaps what he sows. If he sows in the field of his unspiritual nature, he will reap from it a harvest of corruption; but if he sows in the field of the spirit, he will reap from it a harvest of eternal life.[6]

Hell is a concomitant of our present mode of living; it becomes frighteningly real if we die never having had any concern for anyone other than ourselves.

Upon Reflection

> They are not in hell because Father, Son, and Holy Ghost are angry with them, and so cast them into a punishment which their wrath had contrived for them; but they are in wrath and darkness because they have done to the Light which infinitely flows forth from God, as that man doth to the light of the sun, who puts out his own eyes.
> William Law, *An Appeal to all that Doubt*[7]

> Grant us, Lord, the wisdom and the grace to use aright the time that is left to us here on earth. Lead us to repent of our sins, the evil we have done and the good we have not done; and strengthen us to follow the steps of your Son, in the way that leads to the fullness of eternal life; through Jesus Christ our Lord. Amen.
> Funeral Services of *The Alternative Service Book 1980*

> Learning to die means no longer to hate or be burdened with fear. To learn to die means to be caught up in a great chorus that affirms life; that is what faith is. The more we learn to live in freedom from fear the

more we learn to die in freedom from fear. The more we are united to that love with which we know ourselves to be at one, the more immortal we are. As Christians we know that death always lies behind us; it is love that lies ahead.

Dorothee Soelle, *The Inward Road and the Way Back*[8]

Ask now what hell is? It is nature destitute of the Light and Spirit of God and full only of its own darkness; nothing else can make it to be hell. Ask what heaven is? It is nature quickened, enlightened, blessed, and glorified by the Light and Spirit of God dwelling in it.

There is hidden also in the depth of your nature the root or possibility of all the hellish nature, spirit, and tempers of the fallen angels. For heaven and hell have each of them their foundation within us, they come not into us from without, but spring up in us according as our will and heart is turned either to the Light of God or the kingdom of darkness. But when this life, which is in the midst of these two eternities, is at an end, either an angel or a devil will be found to have a birth in us.

William Law, *The Spirit of Prayer*[9]

The will is that which has all power; it unites all that is united in heaven or on earth, it divides and separates all that is divided in nature; it makes heaven, and it makes hell; for there is no hell but where the will of the creature is turned from God, nor any heaven but where the will of the creature works with God.

William Law, *The Way to Divine Knowledge*[10]

I know of no hell, either here or hereafter, but the power and working of wrath, nor any heaven but where the God of Love is all in all, and the working Life of all.

William Law, *The Spirit of Love*[11]

16

The mystical walk: our way in Christ

The love of God encompasses everything within itself and everything that is rooted in love stems from God. (Madame Guyon, *A Short and Easy Method of Prayer*)

It is evident that human nature is very constant in its emotional reactions, whatever religious loyalty it may profess. In its juvenile state it insists on being right, which means that all other opinions and views are wrong. Those who hold them should either be converted to the truth or else be shunned, if not actually destroyed. If one considers the founders of the major world faiths, their total humanity is obvious: Jesus, Gautama, Mohammed, Zoroaster, Lao Tzu, Confucius ... Of the founders of the vast Hindu religion one is less certain. Is Krishna, the incarnation of Vishnu, a human being or merely a legendary figure? In the Hindu Trinity there are Brahma, Vishnu and Siva. But the same query hangs over the identity of Jesus: a brilliant Jewish boy, or only Son of God, or again both?

The wise person ceases to be arrested by such vain speculations and enters into spiritual communion with the minds of such great leaders and the minds of their disciples who extended the primal vision with an enhanced understanding of the world in and on which they and we all live during our brief span of incarnation. Of what happened before, to us personally, we are ignorant, as we are also of what we may expect when we leave our physical body behind. The nature of time is possibly the greatest mystery; one feels it exists as a conceptual state of the mind rather like sight, hearing and thought, but having no independent existence.

It is certain that our inner lives are constantly being modified by the world around us. This includes not only our fellow humans, other creatures, plants and micro-organisms, but also our comparatively small world which we call the solar system (comprising the Sun, Mercury, Venus, Earth, Mars, Jupiter, Saturn, Uranus, Neptune and Pluto with their various satellites or moons). This world is but a minute particle of a total universe so vast as to be beyond human conception.

And even this is not the end: interpenetrating and extending the visible and comprehensible is the endless realm of psychic reality where the soul operates, and its highest point is spiritual sublimity where God is fully known. And yet the divine informs every particle of matter, however lowly it may appear to the precocious human being. The totality is called the cosmos, and Christians of a mystical nature see an aspect of Jesus as one in majesty reigning over the cosmos. This is called the cosmic Christ.

When one enters the mind of Christ – a very different matter from considering it from a distance, albeit ever so reverently – one's own personality expands to the magnitude of the cosmos. It is as if one is in the spacious realm of God, where love reigns effortlessly with justice, strength with humility, beauty with maturity, growth with wisdom. Each quality unfolds to its full magnitude, in this action serving to illuminate the others. God has been described by mystics of the stature of Nicholas of Cusa, as the coincidence of opposites; in the mind of Christ all things *are* together, as a result of God's love. The one thing magnifies the other so that each moves beyond its formal limits to extend the glory of the whole. By being uniquely oneself one becomes effortlessly the other also, because each one bears the divine imprint, which becomes unmistakably real when one actualizes one's own personality.

The great paradox of the spiritual life is identity in difference. The way, indeed the only effective way, of establishing one's identity is to flow effortlessly in the stream of life, giving ungrudgingly of oneself moment by moment and receiving in the same action. There is no special gratitude, but a certain feeling of constant satisfaction that one is a small link in the endless chain of life. The apparent duration of the process is the measure of our own life – we know when it started, at the time of our birth (or more precisely when we attained self-awareness) and we know that it will end when our body dies – but the process continues forever onwards, like a train with many brief halts but no earthly destination.

We have already (in chapter 4) considered Jesus' dictum that no one can serve God and Money, yet money as a metonym for the desirable things of the world is essential for life, let alone satisfaction. The important distinction lies in our attitude to material substance. It should not be served, in which case it becomes our master. But neither should we become its dictator, for it comes from God and has its own integrity. It too deserves care and respect, not simply because it is of variable use to us, but because it reveals something of the divine, even if it is quite repulsive to us.

This does not mean that we, at this moment, are to live together like one extended happy family. Noxious organisms, savage animals and poisonous plants have to be severely isolated or even eliminated. The same reasoning applies to criminals, except that capital punishment ought to be unnecessary. In fact, the purpose of the intrinsically destructive elements of life is to strengthen the more moderate ones. This process of strengthening is physical with reference to what we call, in lordly fashion, 'the lower elements of life', but in human consciousness the process assumes a moral dimension that ascends to spiritual heights as the awareness of God dominates all life.

The spiritual hierarchy of life is a challenging enigma, but it cannot be evaded. In an amazing encounter a friend visited an Indian ashram. He was so lost in spiritual ecstasy that he failed to observe the close proximity of a cobra. When the unwelcome visitor made his presence felt, the disciple was petrified. He was rendered completely speechless. And then from the shadows there emerged a small, unobtrusive figure whose arm had been severely destroyed by cancer. Nevertheless, he approached the venomous creature, lifted it up in his arms and deposited it gently on the surrounding vegetation. The disciple looked on with amazement, not only at the man's equanimity but also at the reptile's passivity. The teacher lifted up his hand to the disciple with compassionate severity and said, 'You did not love him enough.'

This is the way towards accepting noxious forms of life: love conquers everything, but the first on the list to be overcome is oneself. It is worth meditating on Jesus' teaching in the Sermon on the Mount:

> You have heard that they were told, 'Love your neighbour and hate your enemy.' But what I tell you is this: Love your enemies and pray for your persecutors; only so can you be children of your heavenly

Father, who causes the sun to arise on good and bad alike, and sends the rain on the innocent and the wicked.[1]

How does one set about obeying this great commandment? The way forward is to enter into profound wordless meditation as described in chapter 12 and immerse yourself totally in those aspects of your memory that you find especially forbidding. Get to know your full self in the intimacy of silence. Be as judgemental as you can, and do not attempt to forgive yourself. On the contrary, let your history be your prosecutor and your indictment.

At first the process may be intolerably painful, but it is better if the work can be done without outside assistance. There is, however, invariably internal assistance, the Spirit of God who dwells as a conscious presence in us all, no matter how terribly we have denied him in our life up to this juncture. Indeed, until we are isolated from all outside help we will never know the full force of God, because our attention will remain occupied with worldly matters. When these have been completely shut out, the Holy Spirit will begin to lighten our inner darkness just as the sun's rays illuminate the darkness of the night when day breaks at dawn.

As the Spirit illuminates our unhappy mind obsessed with destructive thoughts, so we will automatically relax and find that the thoughts are losing their grip. While still very much with us, they become merely interesting relics of our past life. We no longer need to be defensive about ourselves nor to prove we are always right. We can, on the contrary, let go of our self-centredness and become available to listen and to empathize with all manner of people. In this way Jesus' commandment that we should love our enemies and pray for our persecutors becomes not merely possible but fully attainable. If we cease to react negatively to those who are genuinely hostile to us (as opposed to those whom we fear for personal reasons, and then project that fear on to them as hostility towards ourselves), there is a strong possibility that their hostility will lessen. They may attain a neutral attitude which may even mature into friendship. In this work we should be true to ourselves and not adopt unnaturally friendly poses to obtain a desirable end.

In chapter 8 the dictum quoted was, 'Perfect love banishes fear.'[2] Perfect love can be given out to others only when we love ourselves perfectly. 'God is love; he who dwells in love is dwelling in God, and God in him.'[3] In this sequence we see how fear for personal reasons can be healed – by the same mechanism as that indicated above, except that we should immerse ourselves totally in the fear rather than a forbidding thought. In either case we will experience divine assistance, provided that we let go and trust. This is the faith that leads to healing.

The value of pursuing this course of inner growth unaided has been stressed, but this is only one aspect of a person's life. There should also be favoured interests to lighten what, at least in the early part of the work, may be too arduous. One is certainly not completely isolated from the world, but one now has time for one's own deliberations in silence. This time should dominate one's life at the start of the work.

Our way in Christ does not consist in punctiliously following a moral code. Such a code, typified by the Ten Commandments,[4] is a magnificent introduction to the Good Life, but it gives very little indication of how it may be attained. That it is not the final word can be demonstrated by studying the Sermon on the Mount.[5] This body of spiritual teaching, surely the greatest in existence, does not negate the Ten Commandments, but it extends and expands them to a way of life that can proceed to their attainment in the present moment. To incarnate that assent is the true purpose of our life, but the vast majority of people remain stuck on the material details. However, there is a skilful way of trying to serve God and money; the master is God, but material substance can be of great help in our service to God if it is treated with reverence and shared generously.

Therefore rejoice in all aspects of life, learning from the unpleasant as well as the pleasant. Material existence is an illusion, except in the vision of God. Outside that vision we can say quite humorously, 'Here today, gone tomorrow!' One does not *believe* in God, one *knows* him by experience; and that experience makes all life's vicissitudes worth while. For the end is glorious, primarily for oneself, but as one grows, so one's vision expands to include all humanity and ultimately all that lives.

There is little doubt that individuals are on different planes of spiritual development. Some people are illiterate when compared with the masters of theatre and philosophy of the pre-Christian Greek era, to say nothing of contemporary humanistic thought or scientific endeavour. Religious dogmatism tends to fall midway between these two extremes. A well-known admonition in the Sermon on the Mount is extremely apposite in this context: 'Do not give dogs what is holy; do not throw your pearls to the pigs; they will only trample on them, and turn and tear you to pieces.'[6] Only when all the relevant information is at hand can one assess the probable truth of a situation.

A topical example is the research of Dr Ian Stevenson into the question of reincarnation. A scientist of sterling integrity, one can accept his findings from a number of countries that affirm this way of progress in the afterlife; but one has to admit that the number of suggestive cases he quotes is minuscule compared with the vast populations of these countries. Only relatively few people can assimilate the concept of reincarnation in a responsible manner. Most will feel pride at a past triumph or devastating shame at a past failure. In fact, we can only act in the place where we now stand. The most that can be said in favour of memories of the past that might relate to the concept of reincarnation is that they keep us on the straight and narrow path of moral action. That examples of outstanding genius may be related to experience in past lives is an intriguing, but as yet unproven, hypothesis. Opinions often change in the face of more evidence; dogmatic assertions have been proved wrong on more than one occasion in the past.

'I have come that they may have life, and may have it in all its fullness.'[7] Whether these words come directly from the Master or are in fact a statement of the unknown writer of the fourth Gospel is immaterial. In fact, such a glowing testimony to the Light is more eloquent proof than the Light's own brightness. Life in all its fullness! It is inconceivable that anyone who has set foot on the earth has known it; the supreme mystics have come closest to it when they have experienced the beatific vision: the dissolution of material substance and the revelation of endless peace in which the heart of all creation flows in perfect concord. This peace is God's eternal manifestation. 'Peace is my parting gift to you, my own peace, such as the world cannot give. Set your troubled hearts at rest, and banish your fears.'[8]

This is the end of the spiritual path, which paradoxically is endless. It is fitting that the word 'end' has two distinct meanings: conclusion and purpose. The beatific vision is the purpose of each individual's life and the conclusion of it. In fact, only people of the stature of Jesus and Gautama can achieve it in one lifetime, if indeed they too have not been groomed by God in a previous existence for their great work among us. This work too is endless; the only conceivable conclusion and purpose is the deification of all life, with the human figure in the vanguard.

Upon Reflection

It is his will that we have knowledge of four things. The first is that he is the foundation from whom we have our life and our being. The second is that he protects us mightily and mercifully, during the time that we are in our sin, among all our enemies who are so fierce against us; and we are in so much more peril because we give them occasion for this, and we do not know our own need. The third is how courteously he protects us and makes us know that we are going astray. The fourth is how steadfastly he waits for us, and does not change his demeanour, for he wants us to be converted and united to him in love, as he is to us.

Julian of Norwich, *Revelations of Divine Love*[9]

Let us then not be afraid to apply Paul's principle of praising God for everything to thanking him for permitting our sins. He has not allowed them beyond the extent to which he can turn them into good. Though frozen hard as fact in history, our sins remain fluid in what they may yield as value in the present.

They serve to remind us of our frailty, of our constant need for God, and of the enduring nature of his love which will never desert us however grievously we fall. In praising God for the past lies acceptance, and in acceptance lies healing, and in this context healing especially from guilt-ridden memories.

We may bring these thoughts to their end (and climax) by quoting Julian's memorable words from the closing chapter of her book:

When judgement is given and we are all brought up above, then we shall see clearly the secrets now hidden from us. In that day not one of us will want to say, 'Lord, if it had been done this way, it would have been well done.' But we shall all say with one voice, 'Lord, blessed may you be, for it is so, and it is well. And now we see truly that all things were done as it was ordained before anything was made.'

Robert Llewelyn, *Our Duty and our Joy*[10]

Notes

Chapter 1

1 William Blake, *Auguries of Innocence*.
2 *The Cloud of Unknowing*, (Classics of Western Spirituality, Paulist Press, 1981) chapter 6, p. 130.
3 2 Corinthians 6.10.
4 Exodus 20.4–5.
5 Exodus 20.7.
6 G. Moreton, *The Works of the Revd W. Law, MA* (London, 1893), vol. 8, pp. 1–2.
7 Ibid., vol. 7, p. 234.

Chapter 2

1 Matthew 5–7.
2 Romans 6.23.
3 Acts 5.38–9.
4 Matthew 8.28–34.
5 Matthew 12.1–8.
6 Matthew 12.9–14.
7 Matthew 22.15–22.
8 Matthew 21.9.
9 Matthew 27.22–3.
10 Matthew 10.2–4.
11 John 13–17.
12 Mark 14 contains all these allusions.
13 Mark 15 contains all these allusions.
14 Luke 24.13–32.
15 Matthew 8.23–7.
16 Matthew 14.13–21 and 15.32–9.
17 Matthew 14.22–33.

18   Matthew 21.12–13.
19   Matthew 27.46.
20   G. Moreton, *Works of W. Law*, vol. 7, p. 108.
21   Alan Watts, *Behold the Spirit* (Vintage Books, 1971), pp. 74–5.
22   Moreton, op. cit., vol. 8, p. 74.
23   Ibid., vol. 7, p. 110.

Chapter 3

1   Genesis 1.2.
2   Exodus 36.1.
3   Deuteronomy 34.9.
4   Judges 14.6.
5   Isaiah 61.1.
6   Psalm 51.11.
7   Isaiah 11.2.
8   Isaiah 42.1.
9   Ezekiel 36.26; Joel 2.28–9.
10   Wisdom 7.7; 9.17.
11   Mark 1.10.
12   Mark 1.12–13.
13   Luke 1.35.
14   John 14.16.
15   Philippians 1.19; Romans 8.9; Galatians 4.6.
16   Romans 8.9–11.
17   Romans 8.26.
18   1 Corinthians 2.9–16.
19   1 Corinthians 7.40.
20   Romans 8.23.
21   Matthew 7.21–3.
22   Galatians 5.22–3.
23   1 Corinthians 12.28.
24   1 Corinthians 14.19.
25   Isaiah 55.8.
26   Simone Weil, *Gravity and Grace* (Ark, 1987), p. 106.
27   Olivier Clément, *The Roots of Christian Mysticism* (English edn: New City, 1993), p. 89.
28   Walter Hilton (trans. Leo Shirley-Price), *The Ladder of Perfection* (Penguin, rev. edn 1988), p. 209.
29   Martin Israel, *Christ, Son of God* (Churches Fellowship for Psychical and Spiritual Studies, 1982), p. 10.

Chapter 4

1 John 18.38.
2 John 18.31.
3 John 18.36–7.
4 Francis Bacon (1561—1626), *Essays* 'Of Truth'.
5 Genesis 1.20–27.
6 Genesis 2.8–14.
7 Lamentations 1.1–2.
8 As referred to in Hebrews 9.22.
9 Jeremiah 31.31.
10 Isaiah 53.5, 12.
11 Mark 1.4, 15.
12 Matthew 9.13.
13 Mark 10.45.
14 Luke 22.20; 1 Corinthians 11.25.
15 Matthew 26.28.
16 Luke 22.37.
17 John 1.29.
18 John 19.14, 36.
19 1 Corinthians 15.3.
20 Acts 8.32–5.
21 Colossians 1.20.
22 Romans 3.25.
23 1 Peter 1.19.
24 St Athanasius, *De Incarnatione*, 54.
25 Isaiah 1.10–17; Hosea 6.6.
26 Hebrews 10.31.
27 Matthew 6.24.
28 Julian of Norwich (*c.* 1342–after 1413) (trans. Clifton Walters) *Revelations of Divine Love* (Penguin, 1966), ch. 27, p.103.
29 1 John 4.18.
30 1 John 4.16.
31 G. Moreton, *Works of W. Law*, vol. 8, p. 85.
32 *Theologia Germanica*, a late fourteenth-century mystical treatise.
33 G. Moreton, op. cit., vol. 8, pp. 125–6.

Chapter 5

1 Hebrews 11.1–40.
2 Hebrews 12.1–6.
3 Matthew 13.54–8.
4 Matthew 24.6–8.

5 *The Philokalia* (Faber and Faber, 1990), vol. 2, p. 308.
6 Julia Gatta, *A Pastoral Art* (Darton, Longman & Todd, 1987), pp. 32–3.
7 Walter Hilton (trans. Leo Shirley-Price), *The Ladder of Perfection* (Penguin, 1957), p. 198.
8 G. Moreton, *Works of W. Law*, vol. 5, p. 117.
9 Ibid., vol. 5, p. 153.

Chapter 6

1 Romans 8.18 and Colossians 1.24.
2 Matthew 7.21–3.
3 Julian of Norwich, *Showings* (Paulist Press, 1978), ch. 48.
4 Ibid., ch. 37.
5 Ibid., ch. 56.
6 Ibid., ch. 27.
7 Ibid., ch. 32.
8 Ibid., ch. 39.
9 Ibid., ch. 47.
10 Ibid., ch. 40.

Chapter 7

1 Matthew 16.26.
2 Matthew 5.39.
3 Matthew chapters 5–7.
4 Matthew 19.26.
5 Matthew 26.47–50.
6 Matthew 27.3–10.
7 1 Thessalonians 5.17 (Authorized Version).
8 G. Moreton, *Works of W. Law*, vol. 7, p. 110.
9 In George Appleton, *The Practice of Prayer* (Mowbray, 1979).
10 Mme Jeanne-Marie de la Motte Guyon (trans. Thomas Digby Brooke), *A Short and Easy Method of Prayer* (Hodder, 1990), p. 51.
11 In Oliver Clément, *The Roots of Christian Mysticism* (English edition: New City, 1993), p. 115.
12 Ibid., pp. 116–17.
13 Brian Wren (1936–). From the hymn, 'Lord God, your love has called us here'. Copyright © 1975, 1995 Hope Publishing Company for the USA, Canada, Australia and New Zealand and Stainer & Bell Ltd, London for all other territories.

Chapter 8

1 Deuteronomy 18.10–14.
2 Jeremiah 31.31–4; Ezekiel 36.26.
3 1 Corinthians 13.8.
4 Madame Guyon, op. cit., pp. 23, 81–2.
5 G. Moreton, *Works of W. Law*, vol. 7, pp. 132–4.

Chapter 9

1 Matthew 19.24.
2 1 Corinthians 13.11.
3 Acts 17.28.
4 Matthew 7.1.
5 Romans 8.28.
6 1 John 4.18.
7 John 15.13.
8 Matthew 18.20.
9 In Robert Llewelyn (ed.), *Fire of Divine Love* (Burns and Oates, 1995), p. 76.
10 *The Philokalia* (Faber and Faber, 1990), vol. 2, p. 148.

Chapter 10

1 John 2.23–5.
2 Acts 2.14–47.
3 Acts 3 and 4.1–2.
4 Luke 23.35–7 and parallel passages in Mark 15.29–32 and Matthew 27.39–44.
5 Matthew 27.46 and Mark 15.34.
6 Matthew 6.24.
7 *Hamlet,* Act 1 Scene 3, 78–80.
8 Matthew 6.26–34.
9 Colossians 1.27.
10 Dag Hammarskjöld, (trans. Leif Sjoberg and W.H. Auden), *Markings* (Faber and Faber, 1964), pp. 147–8.
11 In Elizabeth Bassett, *Love is My Meaning* (Darton Longman and Todd, 1986), pp. 51–2.

Chapter 11

1 *Hamlet,* Act 3 Scene 1, 60.
2 Mark 15.34–9.
3 Luke 23.34.

4 Matthew 18.21–2.
5 Romans 3.23.
6 Luke 15.11–32.
7 Matthew 11. 28–30.
8 Hammarskjöld, *op. cit.*, p. 197.
9 From the hymn, 'Dear Lord and Father of mankind'.
10 In Llewelyn (ed.), *Fire of Divine Love*, (Burns and Oates, 1995), p. 54.

Chapter 12

1 W. R. Inge, *Studies of English Mystics* (Murray, 1906).
2 Maximus the Confessor (trans. George Berthold), *Selected Writings* (Paulist Press, 1985), pp. 43, 45.
3 Walter Hilton, *The Ladder of Perfection* (Penguin, 1988), p. 167.
4 G. Moreton, *Works of W. Law*, vol. 7, p. 211.

Chapter 13

1 Luke 10.25–37.
2 Matthew 7.21.
3 David Martin, *Modern Believing* (the journal of the Modern Church-people's Union), in the chapter 'Christianity: Converting and Converted', 2000, *vol., 14* p. 13.
4 Acts 2.38, 40.
5 Acts 2.44–5.
6 Karl Marx, *Criticism of the Gotha Programme*, 1875, ch. 29, p. 14.
7 Karl Marx, in the Introduction to *Criticism of Hegel's Philosophy of Right*.
8 Acts 2. 46–7.
9 An earlier reference to this prayer is found in *The Cloud of Unknowing* by an anonymous English Christian mystic.
10 *Phaedo*, 67C.
11 In Robert Llewelyn (ed.), *An Oratory of the Heart: Daily Readings with Brother Lawrence* (Darton, Longman & Todd, 1984), p. v.
12 Ibid., p. 2.
13 Luke 9.25.
14 Acts 9.1–25.
15 Acts 13.9–12.
16 Luke 15.11–31.
17 In R. Llewelyn (ed.), *Fire of Divine Love* (Burns and Oates, 1995), p. 117.
18 In R. Llewelyn (ed.), *An Oratory of the Heart* (Darton, Longman and Todd, 1984), p. 9.
19 In Llewelyn (ed.), *Fire of Divine Love*, (Burns and Oates, 1995), p. 87.
20 Robert Llewelyn, *Our Duty and our Joy* (Darton, Longman & Todd, 1996), p. 40.

Chapter 14

1 John 1.1–5 (Authorized Version).
2 John 1.9–14 (Authorized Version).
3 Psalm 33.6.
4 1 Samuel 15.10; Isaiah 55.11; Jeremiah 23.29.
5 Wisdom of Solomon 9.1–2, 18.15.
6 John 1.1 and 14; 1 John 1.1; Revelation 19.13.
7 Matthew 18.20.
8 2 Corinthians 11.14, 15.
9 See chapter 7.
10 Colossians 1.27.
11 Matthew 7.18–19.
12 Galatians 5.22–3.
13 Dietrich Bonhoeffer, *Letters and Papers from Prison* (Collins Fontana, 1959), pp. 123, 125.
14 Bernard Bro (trans. Alan Neame), *The Little Way* (Darton, Longman & Todd, 1979), p. 26.
15 Jean Lafrance, *My Vocation is Love: Thérèse of Lisieux* (St Paul Publications, 1990), p. 170.
16 John Nelson (ed.), *The Arms of Love, with St Thérèse of Lisieux* (Darton, Longman & Todd, 1997), p. 39.
17 In Olivier Clément, *The Roots of Christian Mysticism* (trans. Theodore Berkeley) (New City, 1993), p. 251.
18 Ibid., p. 249.
19 Ibid., p. 271.

Chapter 15

1 Matthew 25.30.
2 Matthew 25.11–12.
3 Matthew 25.41, 46.
4 Matthew 6.9–10.
5 Romans 3.23–4.
6 Galatians 6.7–8.
7 In G. Moreton, *Works of W. Law*, vol. 6, p. 129.
8 Dorothee Soelle, *The Inward Road and the Way Back* (Darton, Longman and Todd, 1979), pp. 13–14.
9 In G. Moreton, op. cit., vol. 7, p. 33.
10 Ibid., vol. 7, p. 217.
11 Ibid., vol. 8, p. 38.

Chapter 16

1 Matthew 5.43–5.
2 1 John 4.18.
3 1 John 4.16.
4 Exodus 20.1–17.
5 Matthew 5–7.
6 Matthew 7.6.
7 John 10.10.
8 John 14.27.
9 Julian of Norwich, *Revelations of Divine Love*, ch. 78.
10 Robert Llewelyn, *Our Duty and our Joy* (Darton, Longman & Todd, 1996), p. 25.

Further reading and resources

Basset, Elizabeth, *The Bridge is Love* (Darton, Longman & Todd, 1981).
Jean-Pierre de Caussade, *Self-Abandonment to Divine Providence* (Fontana, 1971).
Clément, Olivier, *The Roots of Christian Mysticism* (English edn: New City, 1993).
Guyon, Mme Jeanne-Marie de la Motte, *A Short and Easy Method of Prayer* (Hodder, 1990).
Happold, F.C., *The Journey Inwards* (Darton, Longman & Todd, 1968).
——, *Mysticism* (Penguin, 1970).
Israel, Martin, *Life Eternal* (SPCK, 1993).
John, Jeffrey, *This is our Faith* (Redemptorist, 1999).
Lawrence, Brother, *The Practice of the Presence of God* (Oneworld, 1993).
Llewelyn, Robert, *Our Duty and our Joy* (Darton, Longman and Todd, 1996).
Llewelyn, Robert (ed.), *Daily Readings with Brother Lawrence* (Darton, Longman & Todd, 1984).
——(ed.), *Daily Readings with Jean-Pierre de Caussade* (Darton, Longman & Todd, 1984).
——(ed.), *Daily Readings with Julian of Norwich* (Darton, Longman & Todd, 1984).
——(ed.), *Daily Readings with William Law* (Templegate, 1987).
Moreton, G., (ed.), *The Works of the Revd. W. Law, MA*, vols. 5–9 (London, 1892–3).
Nicholl, Donald, *Holiness* (Darton, Longman & Todd, 1987).
——, *The Testing of Hearts* (Marshall Morgan and Scott, 1989).
Nouwen, Henri, *With Open Hands* (Ave Maria Press, 1975).
Vanstone, W.H., *Love's Endeavour, Love's Expense* (Darton, Longman & Todd, 1977).
Woolley, John, *I am with You* (Crown, 1991).

Websites

http://ccel.wheaton.edu   The Christian Classics Ethereal Library has a great
                           many classic Christian texts that may be down-
                           loaded for private use.

www.abebooks.com   These are three excellent sites for obtaining
www.alibris.com   out-of-print books.
www.bibliofind.com

www.martinisrael.com

'One does not believe in God; one knows him by experience, and that experience makes all life's vicissitudes worthwhile. For the end is glorious [and] as one grows so one's vision expands to include all humanity and ultimately all that lives.'

In *Learning to Love*, Martin Israel explores the question How can we learn to obey the commandment to love our neighbour? Through powerful meditations on the nature of existence he illuminates the 'mystical walk' that ends in love.

Martin Israel gave up a career as a distinguished pathologist in the early 1970s, converted to Christianity and became an ordained priest in the Church of England. From his first book, *Summons to Life*, onwards he has explored the mysteries of love and the Spirit.

Cover design: Richard Carr
Cover photograph © Corbis

£7.99

MOWBRAY
A Continuum imprint
London • New York
www.continuumbooks.com

PRINTED IN GREAT BRITAIN
ISBN 0-264-67529-0

9 780264 675299 >